P9-DMZ-445

FAIL FAST OR WIN BIG

Fail Fast or Win Big

THE START-UP PLAN FOR STARTING NOW

Bernhard Schroeder

ⱵAMACOM

American Management Association

New York • Atlanta • Brussels • Chicago • Mexico City • San Francisco
Shanghai • Tokyo • Toronto • Washington, D. C.

Ketchikan Public Library
Ketchikan, AK 99901

Bulk discounts available. For details visit:
www.amacombooks.org/go/specialsales
Or contact special sales:
Phone: 800-250-5308
Email: specialsls@amanet.org
View all the AMACOM titles at: www.amacombooks.org
American Management Association: www.amanet.org

This publication is designed to provide accurate and authoritative information in regard to the subject matter covered. It is sold with the understanding that the publisher is not engaged in rendering legal, accounting, or other professional service. If legal advice or other expert assistance is required, the services of a competent professional person should be sought.

The LeanModel Framework is a registered trademark of the author.

Library of Congress Cataloging-in-Publication Data
Schroeder, Bernhard.
    Fail fast or win big : the start-up plan for starting now / Bernhard Schroeder.—
First Edition.
        pages cm
    Includes bibliographical references and index.
    ISBN 978-0-8144-3478-9 (hardcover) — ISBN 0-8144-3478-9 (hardcover) —
ISBN 978-0-8144-3479-6 (ebook) — ISBN 0-8144-3479-7 (ebook) 1. New business
enterprises—Planning. 2. New products. I. Title.
    HD62.5.S3547 2015
    658.1'1--dc23
                                                                    2014027516

© 2015 Bernhard Schroeder.
All rights reserved.
Printed in the United States of America.

This publication may not be reproduced, stored in a retrieval system, or transmitted in whole or in part, in any form or by any means, electronic, mechanical, photocopying, recording, or otherwise, without the prior written permission of AMACOM, a division of American Management Association, 1601 Broadway, New York, NY 10019.

The scanning, uploading, or distribution of this book via the Internet or any other means without the express permission of the publisher is illegal and punishable by law. Please purchase only authorized electronic editions of this work and do not participate in or encourage piracy of copyrighted materials, electronically or otherwise. Your support of the author's rights is appreciated.

About AMA
American Management Association (www.amanet.org) is a world leader in talent development, advancing the skills of individuals to drive business success. Our mission is to support the goals of individuals and organizations through a complete range of products and services, including classroom and virtual seminars, webcasts, webinars, podcasts, conferences, corporate and government solutions, business books, and research. AMA's approach to improving performance combines experiential learning—learning through doing—with opportunities for ongoing professional growth at every step of one's career journey.

Printing number
10 9 8 7 6 5 4 3 2 1

For my children **Nigel**, **Britney**, and **Haley**, and
for entrepreneurs everywhere . . . do or do not. Be happy.

Contents

FAIL FAST OR WIN BIG

Why Today's Entrepreneurs Need to Read This Book

Fail Fast or Win Big is not about failing. It's about embracing a new way of thinking about creating and launching a company. In the start-up world today, you can't spend months writing a complex business plan that will be out of date before your idea ever comes to market. There is no time to create the perfect company on paper before testing it in the real world. And you don't have to, either—not with new sources of capital, such as crowdfunding, waiting to be exploited.

You still need to acquire a deep understanding of the marketplace and your customers so that you are more knowledgeable than your potential competitors, but you also have to beat them to the punch. You are much better off launching a minimally viable product or service, one that satisfies your core customers' needs, and adjusting it on the fly after you see what's attractive about it and what isn't. Fortunately, the tools are available now to let you get started in 90 days, if not less; after all, your time is the most important investment you make. If your product or service doesn't work out, you've saved yourself plenty to win big with the next idea.

The LeanModel Framework will help you move as fast as you need to go. It's the culmination of my work with some of the most talented people in the world during the past 20 years. Some of those people were fellow professionals in our integrated marketing agency, CKS | Partners, which grew very fast, accelerated through an initial public offering (IPO), and then was sold two years later for more than $300 million. Other people I met through "corporate entrepreneurship" where, working together, we spun out divisions and/or new products and services very rapidly. The last group I was in consisted of entrepreneurs launching start-ups, mostly on the West Coast.

While everyone seems to recognize the end result when companies become successful, almost no one remembers the lean days that usually preceded that success. That's when these companies were started in homes, garages, warehouses, and on college campuses. Looking back now, I see that almost all these successful companies embraced a LeanModel Framework: building a solid business model, utilizing lean resources, rapidly prototyping a minimally viable product, and then seeking customer feedback. With that feedback, they then pivoted, evolved, or abandoned the idea.

The philosophy behind the LeanModel Framework is one I adopted early in my own career and that I now espouse as the Director of Programs at the Lavin Entrepreneurship Center, San Diego State University, and as a lecturer for several entrepreneurship courses. Early marketing work in my career with Fortune 500 companies convinced me of two things: (1) Large companies move too slow; and (2) I could not work with slow companies. Instead I looked for opportunities with companies that had a desire to move fast, as they were taking advantage of new market opportunities. I moved away from the General Motors accounts and I embraced the Kellogg's and Nikon assignments that were rapidly prototyping marketing strategies to introduce new products or services, and they were grabbing market share quickly.

When I did work with some automotive companies, I welcomed the chance to help craft new marketing or customer solutions, for smaller, nimbler companies at the time like Hyundai, Mitsubishi, and Mazda. Later, in Silicon Valley, the challenge was to sharpen the education-marketing focus at Apple and define the online marketing strategy for a growing company called Nike. Or, it was taking a small regional craft beer named Widmer and rolling them out nationwide in bottles for the first time ever.

In choosing to work with nimbler, faster-moving companies, I realized it was not about me or my ego. I thrived on the notion of seeing a market opportunity and of moving fast to win big. And I loved working with people who were not afraid to take measured risks in an attempt to win big.

I have worked with some great companies, both large and small. Do you know what made them great, beyond inspirational leadership and usually an amazing culture? It was a powerful sense that they had a meaningful purpose and a destiny, but that in order to fulfill that destiny, they had to move fast. They recognized that moving too slowly would cost them—in terms of either market share or long-term survival. In other words, their core belief was that if they did not move fast, they would ultimately fail.

Let me give you some examples of what the LeanModel Framework looks like in action. In the early 1990s, I was tasked with helping lead a team working with a small start-up called McAfee. The company made anti-virus software, but it was a very small player in a marketplace dominated by larger software companies. As we reviewed potential strategies, we noticed that corporate IT managers routinely looked for additional information or support on bulletin board systems (BBS). These open computer networks allowed people to connect and share information and software solutions. Since this start-up could not afford to package or distribute its software through the traditional distribution channels, we recommended they upload their software to the BBS networks, distribute the software for free (for 30 days), then ask the companies to pay for it after it had been used by their IT employees. This was amazingly successful, and it created a company with more than $2 billion in revenue today. More important, the company's business model and method of distribution changed the way software could be distributed and purchased.

There was another opportunity to help figure out a company's business model back in the early Internet days. We met with the Yahoo! founders when they were still on Stanford's campus, running the early version of Yahoo!'s website on the university's servers. That was a lean start-up. Honestly, we really could not figure out the business model at the time (though they were starting to get a lot of website traffic). One thing we did notice was that the website was not well designed from a user-interface point of view. Not only was the company's branding weak, it was almost impossible to find something quickly, as the website was using way too many links and had poor navigation design.

Yahoo! did not have much money at the time, and they asked us if we would help them in exchange for some equity. We did. We redesigned the user interface and overhauled the website design. During the next six weeks, we created a more powerful, simpler user interface that was more logical and better ordered. But then everyone had an opinion about the new design versus the old design. And everyone was nervous. We convinced the founders to let the customers decide. So, alternating website visitors were served up the new version of the website. Then the next time they visited the website, they received the old version of the website. They were asked to vote on which website design was easier to navigate, and more than 50,000 website visitors voted in the first 72 hours. The majority voted for the new design, much to the founders' dismay. So, we launched the new website, and Yahoo! took off. We then began refining the Yahoo! business model by adding the search function and eventually an advertising model.

This notion of testing products with customers and getting feedback is critical; I call it *customer truth*. Customers are not always right, but they are never wrong.

In the mid-1990s, I had probably my most memorable experience reflecting the mentality of the LeanModel Framework. The founder/entrepreneur of a start-up I'd never heard of called our agency office in Portland, Oregon, in search of a marketing agency and strategic partner to help him grow the business. He had launched a somewhat crude website about six months earlier (a minimally viable product), and it was gaining some traction with customers. So my creative director and I agreed to go to the meeting, which was about three hours away. Driving in what turned out to be a downpour, just terrible weather, I was regretting my decision.

When my creative director and I arrived at the company's location in a seedy part of Seattle, in a rundown warehouse district, my instincts were telling me to leave. We entered the warehouse; there were no real offices, just employees all together in one large room. Water was dripping from the leaky roof. A dog wandered by. The desks were doors mounted on two by four's. It sure looked like no one was spending money on anything. Then we met the founder. He brought us up to date on the past six months, and told us what he needed from us. Which was a lot.

The website and daily operations were working. Orders were coming in every day. They just needed more awareness in their target marketplace. He then explained his big-picture vision. His strategy was to acquire a certain number of customers based on selling one type of product and then, once that happened, sell those same customers many different kinds of products.

I'm not going to lie to you; initially I did not buy the big-picture vision. But I was fascinated by how lean the company was being run and how aggressive it was in trying to improve its business model. We had an amazing meeting. At the very end, the founder asked us if we were seriously interested in changing the world. To be honest, I did not know what that meant. But I knew beyond a shadow of a doubt that this start-up was going to move fast. I had no idea if it would win big, but based on the founder's strategy of grabbing customers quickly, it was either going to win big or fail *really* fast.

As we drove back to our offices, three hours in more rain, we both felt we had just been involved in a meeting that was going to define the usefulness and the potential of the Internet. Win or lose. When he called the next week, we told Jeff Bezos we would work with him. If you are ready to fail fast or win big, read on.

CHAPTER ONE

The End of Business Plans

If you want to sell a product, just make it. If you want to sell a service, just deliver it. If you want to create a company, just create one. There has never been a time like the one we are living in right now.

> *"Move fast and break things. Unless you are breaking stuff, you are not moving fast enough."*
> —Mark Zuckerberg

New products and services are appearing so rapidly that we cannot even see new industries forming until they are already of significant size. The evolution of digital music led to the development of MP3 players, which quickly became just a feature of this new thing called a smartphone, which spawned its own multi-billion-dollar case and accessory industry. And that does not even begin to touch the size and opportunity of the mobile applications industry.

Look anywhere around you. Organic foods, health-care services, GPS-based technologies and products, renting cars by the hour (Zipcar, Car2Go), and the like. Companies are launching and trial-running services and products faster than ever before. As an entrepreneur, you need to accept that *speed to market* is the new normal, and that *fast* just means faster to take advantage of the opportunities that are seemingly nowhere and then everywhere. *Fail Fast or Win Big* will help you understand how you can move faster, how you can learn if you actually have something worthy of being a company, or perhaps how you can evolve, pivot, or abandon the idea.

How do you start, though? Do you write a business plan? Build a prototype? Seek investor capital? And which do you do first? To understand the start-up ecosystem and the need for speed, let's look at how things used to be done and why they no longer work as well anymore.

WHAT'S A BUSINESS PLAN?

A business plan is a formal statement of a set of business goals, the reasons they are believed attainable, and the plan for reaching those goals. It may also contain background information about the organization or team attempting to reach those goals. The business plan is formally written; most detailed business plans average between 25 and 40 written pages. The core sections of a business plan may include the following:

- *Executive Summary.* The first section is a concise overview of your business plan. While the summary should be short, it must be well written. Your objective is to draw readers in so they want to learn more about your company. Though this section appears first, consider writing it last, after you've worked out the details of your plan and can summarize your thoughts clearly.

- *Company Description and Mission.* This high-level view of your company should explain who you are, how you plan to operate, and what your goals are.

- *Products or Services.* This section clearly describes what you are selling, focusing on the customer benefits. It incorporates details about suppliers, product or service costs, and the revenue expected from the sale of that product or service.

- *Marketplace and Competitive Analysis.* Here's where you show your industry and marketplace knowledge, information on the competition, key trends, key insights about your potential customers, and where you make your recommendations.

- *Strategy and Implementation.* This section defines your sales and marketing strategy and detailed tactics; in addition, it indicates key elements of your business operations.

- *Organization and Management Team.* In this section, you outline your company's organizational structure and identify the company owners, management team, and board of directors.

- *Financial Plan and Projections.* This last section of your business plan should be developed with someone who can help you with financial projections, revenue statements, and other financial documentation you may need based on your business model.

I have written quite a few business plans and I have reviewed hundreds of other business plans. However long you think it will take you to write a solid business plan, you have to double or triple that time and effort to include the myriad details and the research data you need to provide.

As much as you think you are writing the business plan for yourself, you are not. The writing of the plan is helpful to you in terms of planning and understanding your potential business, but the plan itself is written for others, who may become partners, employees, and perhaps investors.

WHO NEEDS A BUSINESS PLAN?

We have had entrepreneurs creating and running new companies for centuries. To start and grow initially, they turned to friends and family for funds. If they had collateral, they could apply for a bank loan, which the entrepreneur paid off over time with interest. Then, in the 1960s, venture capitalists created a new way of building an enterprise expressed by this formula:

Entrepreneur opportunity + business plan + venture capital = new company.

Why was this so? Because the corporate managers, scientists, researchers, and engineers who were creating the first tech companies in what would become known as Silicon Valley couldn't get bank loans.

The venture capitalists took equity instead of interest, but like the banks of an earlier time, they also wanted to see a detailed business plan in order to understand the opportunity better and to hedge their risk against potential failure. Slowly, at least in Silicon Valley, potential entrepreneurs became "trained" in the critical elements of creating a start-up company: the formula was to come up with a great idea that had a big market, write a detailed business plan, and then go pitch it to venture capitalists so as to get the money needed to launch the company.

What's really amazing is what occurred next. Universities in the United States in the 1980s, especially MBA programs, began to embrace this same model of how companies should be created and funded, and they began teaching the development of business plans and venture financing in both their undergraduate and graduate programs. At the same time, entrepreneurship education began accelerating on university campuses. So it was for a few generations of students that the novel concept started in the 1960s has become the conventional wisdom.

Is it still wise, though? Do you really need to write a detailed business plan? Does a business plan still have value? Let's look at the pros and cons.

The Pros of a Traditional Business Plan

1. *Valuable Market Research.* The best way to determine whether your start-up idea will work is to see what it looks like on

paper. Business plans follow a fairly standard format for a reason: to spot any missing pieces or potential threats and to have a plan to address the opportunity. You really do need to understand the industry, the marketplace, your potential customers, and the competition.

2. *Key Achievements.* As your day-to-day activity list grows longer, a business plan reminds you of the key milestones that may be critical for determining whether your business start-up succeeds or fails. The constant planning process also tries to ensure that you're still tracking along your plan.

3. *Borrowing Money and Investors.* If your business opportunity needs to borrow money or attract an investment to move on to the next level, you will probably need some sort of written document or presentation. Banks and investors get nervous when you can't show them how you are going to spend the investment money and when you might actually drive some revenue. A business plan somehow makes everyone feel good.

4. *Budgeting and Cash Flow.* Before most entrepreneurs start a company, they may or may not have had experience in managing a decreasing amount of investor or friends and family money. Going through the budgeting process provides some level of reality, although no one is ever quite prepared. The creation of budgets helps expose some hidden costs and highlights some areas that will need to be managed very well to maintain cash flow.

5. *Employees and Goals.* Partners and employees need a good understanding of the business and the future goals if they're going to help you grow the business. Business plans may help employees understand the company's progress, while providing assurances to investors that the project they bought into is still on schedule and on plan.

The Cons of a Traditional Business Plan

1. *You are not selling anything.* Business plans can be projects unto themselves that require a great deal of time, effort, and expertise to complete. Rather than wasting time writing a 30- or 40-page business plan, why not just start selling the product, making deals with key distributors, and getting critical feedback from customers?

2. *Waste of time and "perfect" money.* How many business plans have we read where the written opportunity seems amazing, the research seems flawless, and the budgets and projections just seem perfect? The reality is we know the instant the planning is done that the plan itself is in trouble. Markets, competitors, and customers don't stand still and play nice. How many spreadsheets can you create that will actually lead to a sale?

3. *Flexibility and change is required.* You may have planned for every conceivable outcome in minute detail, but you can't see into the future. It is often the entrepreneurs who are quickest to react who determine which companies succeed and which ones fail. Sticking rigidly to your business plan could actually lead to your company's failure.

4. *The temperature of the water.* Quite simply, you don't know whether your potential idea will succeed or fail until you move into the marketplace. Business plans can give you a great deal of confidence, but only when you start doing business will you know whether your idea is a success.

In summary, you cannot afford to waste time or risk your idea on a perfect set of assumptions. You need to sell something and get customer feedback, so you can make your course corrections and keep running forward. As an entrepreneur, you are not in the business of writing business plans.

WHAT'S WRONG WITH THIS MODEL TODAY?

While this model has worked well during the past 50 years, it now has several problems.

First, the opportunities for entrepreneurs in the world have increased, so there are many more opportunities than there are traditional investors. Also, more individual investors want to invest in start-up companies in all areas, not just technology. Would a traditional venture capital investor invest in a burrito stand? Probably not, but that did not stop Chipotle from becoming a successful company. And some of the new start-ups are moving fast and generating revenue almost immediately. Do they need investor capital? Perhaps not.

> *The traditional entrepreneur's model of finding*
> *an opportunity, writing a business plan, and*
> *pitching to venture capital investors is broken.*

Second, because marketplaces are appearing almost overnight, should you risk a marketplace window's closing because you have to spend four to six months writing a detailed business plan and looking for investors? No.

Third, a business plan is out of date the minute it is finished. While writing a business plan is incredibly useful for really doing the research and planning that's necessary to start a new business, the business environment will have changed during those months it took to write the plan. The industry, the marketplace, the target customer, new innovations, your competition, your team, costs associated with your product or service, what investors are investing in, and so on—all these will have changed.

Fourth, and most important, the business plan's greatest failing is that it takes so much time trying to predict success that it also takes too long for you to fail.

On that note, *failure isn't bad*. The baseball team with the most wins in a season, the 1998 New Yankees, still lost nearly a third of their games. The ballplayer with the highest career batting average, Ty

Cobb, had a failure average of .633. The pitcher with the most wins, Cy Young, also had the most losses, 316, which is more losses than the total wins of all but fifteen other pitchers. How are they failures?

"25% of new businesses fail in the first year . . .
71% by year ten. So, Fail Fast."
—Kaufmann 2012 Study

Maybe we need to "celebrate" failure so that people don't feel a stigma associated with it. In truth, there is no stigma. It's all in your mind. Show me a serial entrepreneur, and chances are he or she has failed quite a few times. What's the difference between that entrepreneur and you? He or she doesn't care. Rather, the individual would passionately pursue something to the point of failure than work a 9-to-5 job doing something that's not exciting or rewarding to that person.

It's a fact that 25 percent of businesses fail in their first year. And 75 percent succeed. Focus on that.

The traditional model of writing a detailed business plan, pitching to investors, and obtaining financing will probably never completely go away. Investors have their role in the entrepreneurship ecosystem for some companies. But for most start-up opportunities in the future, the LeanModel Framework will provide a great hedge for success. Starting quickly with lean resources, developing a business model, rapidly prototyping a product or service, crowdfunding to raise capital (when necessary), and then using customer feedback will get you moving to fail fast or win big. In the next chapter, you'll see how it works.

ENTREPRENEUR INSIGHT

About two years ago, I was working with Andrew, a young entrepreneur who was trying to build an online marketing consultancy specializing in improving small businesses' search engine optimization (SEO) to drive revenue. After almost a year, Andrew was still struggling as sales were low and so he redesigned his website to potentially increase sales. He custom-coded and created several software tools to automate some tasks on his website. He started getting emails not from potential clients but from developers wanting to buy his tools. That week, he figured out how to package and sell the software tools. He re-designed his website again on the next weekend to focus on selling just the software solutions. He had 50 sales the first week. Then 100 sales the next week. Andrew now does more than seven figures in annual revenue per year. Moving fast. Listening to customers.

KEY TAKEAWAY

Create a minimum viable product, using a LeanModel Framework, and be prepared to iterate, evolve, or pivot the product or service based on customer feedback. Listen and move fast.

CHAPTER TWO

The New Way:
The LeanModel Framework

Every generation has its unique elements fostering entrepreneurship. Today it's the many new tools and resources that make it much easier than it used to be to create a company relatively quickly with little investment risk. Cloud-based tools like Shopify or Big Commerce let you build an e-commerce website in less than a week to test a product or service in a targeted marketplace for about $35 a month. App-building tools allow you to rapidly build a mobile application and test it with consumers.

> *"You don't learn to walk by following rules.*
> *You learn by doing and falling over."*
> **—Richard Branson, founder, Virgin Group**

Farmers' markets, independent stores, food trucks, and new types of kiosks and vending machines allow you to rapidly test your idea with a reduction in risk. New crowdfunding platforms allow you to raise capital with little personal risk. It's not about taking your time and overanalyzing opportunities. It's about moving fast.

In addition, the needs of three very different generational groups—baby boomers, gen X, and millennials—are shaping several marketplaces and creating growth in multiple industries, while members of those generations are realizing that how their business lives were supposed to go is no longer the case. Baby boomers have extended their retirement (forced or not) and are looking for ways to leverage their skills and experience. Gen Xers are deep enough into their careers to know that building a "solid career" just does not hold any special meaning anymore. "Follow your passion" is becoming more attractive as a possibility. And millennials, who can't imagine a world where people worked at the same place for 40 years, let alone 40 months, want everything yesterday. These are people primed to take advantage of the new entrepreneurial tools, and the last piece of the puzzle is a simple shift to the mentality of the LeanModel Framework. The investment world is primed for this mentality, too.

I teach several entrepreneurship courses at San Diego State University, one of which is related to developing a business plan/business model for an idea to undergraduate students. In 2009, I was watching the "entrepreneur" marketplace (venture capitalists, angel investors, and entrepreneurs) and could feel that the traditional model of creating a company, which included a detailed business plan, was just becoming irrelevant. It's not that the "planning process" of writing a business plan is not valuable—it is. It's just that time, in the start-up learning and obtaining customer feedback, is precious. You'll spend months or even more than a year to write a plan that no one really wants to read anyway. Investors, or even future partners, just want the opportunity in a nutshell.

At Sequoia Capital, one of the most successful venture capital firms in Silicon Valley, they are asking prospective entrepreneurs to limit their presentations and focus on the most critical information needed to understand the opportunity they are proposing, using a slide format (which ideally limits what an individual can put on a set of slides). In their words, "We like business plans that present a lot of information in as few words as possible. [Our] business plan format is a presentation, with 15–20 slides, is all that's needed."

Here is Sequoia Capital's business plan format, their requirements for their slide presentation, so they get what they believe is important to them:

Company Purpose

Problem and Solution

Why Now?

Market Size

Competition

Product

Business Model

Revenue Model

Team and Financials

That's a whole lot less than a traditional business plan.

Brad Feld, an entrepreneur and venture capitalist, offers his point of view on the value of business plans: "By 1997, when I started investing as a venture capital investor, I was no longer reading business plans. And I don't think I have since then. They have become a historical artifact." This sentiment is echoed by industry professionals and entrepreneurs.

A LEANMODEL FRAMEWORK: THE FUTURE

So, instead of spending months writing a business plan and then looking for investors, who may not give you any money anyway, adopt the LeanModel Framework. The LeanModel Framework is made up of four integrated components: Lean Resources, Business Model, Rapid Prototyping, and Customer Truth. See Figure 2.1.

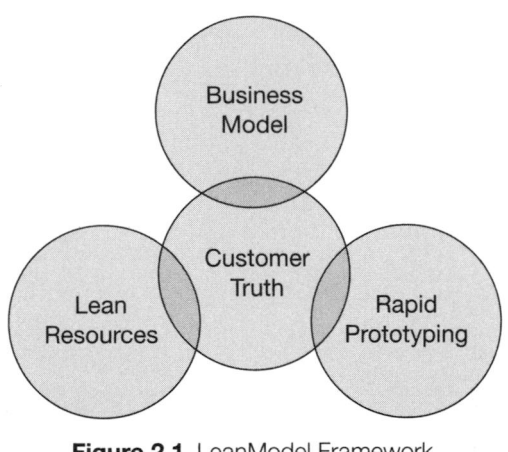

Figure 2.1 LeanModel Framework

Let's take each of these elements in turn:

- *Lean Resources:* Empower a mentality that believes less is more; look to get your company started in the leanest way possible by leveraging everything that you can.

- *Business Model:* Take the time to really understand your marketplace, current trends, and your target customer segment, then craft a business model that not only makes common sense but it makes money.

- *Rapid Prototyping:* If you believe in using lean resources to move fast, then with the same mentality, create a minimum viable product or service that you can test with the marketplace as rapidly as possible.

- *Customer Truth:* Although selecting the right target customer segment is critical, listening to and gathering feedback from your potential customers is crucial. Feedback from customers is what will often give you the insight needed to iterate, pivot, or abandon your idea.

This is the new entrepreneurship model that today's entrepreneurs need to embrace in order to move faster and take advantage of an opportunity. Thus, you'll do more with less by creating a solid business model, rapidly creating a prototype of your product or service to test with customers, using fewer resources, and perhaps utilizing crowdfunding to raise the money you need to move quickly into the marketplace. You'll get customer feedback, make adjustments based on real information instead of projections, and continue to run forward.

If the LeanModel Framework is the rocket ship for entrepreneurs, in Chapter Seven I give you the fuel: crowdfunding. For now, though, let's look at how you might surface an opportunity worth chasing.

ENTREPRENEURS, BE CURIOUS

As a potential entrepreneur, you need to be *manically curious* about a potential product or service—curious to the point you will investigate and research its potential customers, the trends surrounding it, and the marketplace for it. Here's how to get started, based on the experiences of others; this advice will help you gather better information that may actually get you started:

1. *Understand the actual marketplace.* If you have an idea for, let's say, the pet industry, then go visit a pet store and take careful note of the products and services currently offered. Look at online e-commerce pet-care websites and see what their key attributes are.

2. *Talk to the customers.* You can spend all day online or go to the local university library and do research, but there is nothing like talking to customers to get insights. Stand outside of a store and conduct a survey. Visit a dog park or boarding kennel. Learn something about what people want and aren't finding.

3. *Visit your competitors.* If possible, visit your potential competitors and see how they run their businesses. If you have the time, go work for a competitor and learn even more. Look at not only what to do but also what not to do as it relates to customers or the business model.

4. *Understand the key trends.* Pay attention to what is really going on that would affect your marketplace or your customers. In addition to getting key insights via research or trend tracking, consider attending related events or trade shows to learn even more.

5. *Test your idea.* Find a way to test your idea for a product or service even if it's just a prototype or early product. You want to start a food-truck business? Create a taco stand and test your products with real customers. You want to open up a dog kennel? Start a dog-sitting or dog-walking business and learn even more. Have a better idea for new sunglasses with 100 percent recycled materials? Use a local or offshore manufacturer and order 500 pairs. Sell the glasses to local boutiques or create a website and try to sell them online, using key word terms for the search engines to pick your product and direct it to attract the right customers. Learn and adjust.

There are a host of companies that moved into marketplaces and starting selling products to determine if their marketplaces and/or target customers were ready and willing to try something else to meet their needs. Car2Go, a by-the-hour car-sharing service started with a market test in Austin, Texas. When that proved successful, the key managers considered what would be the next city to test-market. They conducted research and reviewed several potential marketplaces. Despite all the research, there was no conclusive data that pointed to one city over another. So they decided to test San Diego, California, on a very small scale. When that proved successful, they grew the operation in San Diego and have now launched in other markets.

In other words, the research will only tell you so much. You have to test to see if your "marketplace timing" is right for a new product or service and if you have targeted the right customer segment. If not, you adjust or abandon the idea. Or, if you are on to something, then you figure out ways to accelerate it. Regardless of your situation, you move faster. You don't have time to write a 30-page business plan. You create a business model on your potential product or service and you go validate it.

THE BUSINESS PLAN IS DEAD;
LONG LIVE THE BUSINESS MODEL

About four years ago, an entrepreneurship professor approached me and asked me if I had heard of a new book that he had recently come across, and he had begun using in his social entrepreneurship course. I hadn't. The book was titled *Business Model Generation*, by Alex Osterwalder and Yves Pigneur. He handed me a copy and told me there was a tool inside called a "business model canvas" that did a great job of helping an entrepreneur to rapidly develop a business model prototype that could be tested quickly with target customers.

"How quickly?" I asked.

He replied, "I have my students creating a business model around an opportunity, getting feedback from 100 potential customers, and iterating the business model in about six weeks." I immediately read the book (learn more at www.businessmodelgeneration.com).

The nagging feeling I had about business plans had just met the reality of a new tool that could rapidly define an opportunity via nine critical business model elements—all on just one page. Traditional business plan or a one-page business model tool? Which one seems simpler to use? Which one can you modify on the fly with customer feedback? Look, some experts would argue, it's just a simple tool. But this simple tool is just what entrepreneurs need to focus on their product or service, and get them to move faster to see if they have something that could win big.

This type of tool allows entrepreneurs to get started quickly, and then if they need to explain the opportunity to, say, Sequoia Capital, they can explain what they learned, describe the size of the opportunity, project the size of the market, relate what lessons have been learned to date, and exclaim how they will make money. All in about 10 to 15 slides.

DOES YOUR BUSINESS HAVE A BUSINESS MODEL?

Many entrepreneurs I meet simply do not take the time to really think through and consider the inner-workings of a start-up opportunity from a business model perspective. This is a critical part of the Lean-Model Framework, however. I will cover the business model and its major components in more detail in the next chapter, but here is a summary of the key elements for you to consider as you shape and iterate a business model for your own start-up.

- *Key Target Customer Segments:* This defines the one or multiple target segments you are targeting with your product or service offering.

- *Value Proposition:* This describes the unique value you are delivering to your customers with your product or service. It's the response to the question: "What problems of our customers are we helping to solve?"

- *Distribution Channels:* You determine your key distribution channels that will deliver your product or service to your potential customers (i.e., online direct, retail, ecommerce partners, etc.).

- *Customer Relationships:* You should be thinking about how to engage with your customers, and how to carry out a long-term relationship with them. If you are dealing with more than one customer segment, you might find a very different type of relationship is required for each. The key question is "What do you want customers to say or feel about your product or service?"

- *Revenue Streams:* You need to identify exactly how you will drive revenue from your product or service (i.e., online sales, retail sales, indirect through partners, licensing, etc.).

- *Key Resources:* This describes the most important assets required to make a business model work and is key in the functioning of all other aspects of the model. What is it you need to actually start and run the business?

- *Key Activities:* These are activities that are crucial in making the business work. You might need to accomplish certain tasks, hire a key person, sign a critical contract, and so on.

- *Key Partnerships:* These describe one's network of suppliers and partners that exist to allow a business to function properly. These could be a key manufacturing supplier, a key distributor, a key technology company, and the like.

- *Cost Structure:* This defines costs that are both direct (related directly to the product or service) and indirect (related to the operations of the business like employees, rent, and any other overhead costs).

In addition to understanding that the world has changed forever and that speed to market is critical, it's important to embrace all the elements of the LeanModel Framework (lean resources, business model, rapid prototyping, and customer truth) so as to take advantage of an opportunity and to move fast and perhaps build an amazing company.

Welcome to your future.

ENTREPRENEUR INSIGHT

About 18 months ago, I was approached by Duncan, an entrepreneur who had just started his third mobile company. He had an idea for a new application that he felt would tap into the mindset and behavior of 14- to 20-year-olds. He had done extensive research, knew the marketplace, and had noted all the key trends. He just did not want to spend $250,000 to build the application (both iPhone and Android versions) without interacting with customers.

How do you test a mobile application when it's not built yet? I encouraged Duncan to design the mobile app in HTML (like a website) to mimic key features and to test the application with students on campus using iPads. By offering an iPad giveaway promotion, he encouraged about 300 students to "play" with the application.

Based on student feedback, Duncan completely changed the features, functionality, and design of the application. Now produced and distributed, it is well on track to do over 2 million downloads in the first year.

KEY TAKEAWAY

You are not in the business of writing business plans. You need to adopt a LeanModel Framework mentality and be willing to learn enough about your opportunity so that you can test your product or service in the marketplace. Rather than spending five to seven months writing a business plan, test something.

CHAPTER THREE

Ideas Are Great but Business Models Rule

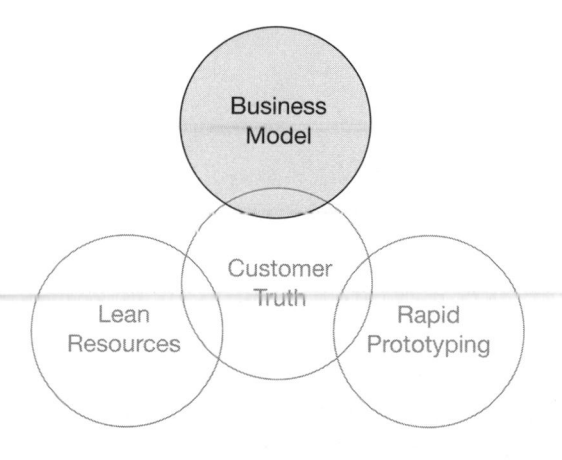

For the majority of entrepreneurs, coming up with an idea or a solution to a problem is what they focus on—to the point of ignoring whether or not there is a solid business model that can be created to support a potential company. This is critical moment for a young start-up. Realizing exactly what is working and what is not working in the context of a business model could likely be the most strategic decisions an entrepreneur can make. Let me give you an example.

Imagine Jeff Bezos looking to create a company called Amazon in the early '90s. He sees book sales on the rise, and the Borders and

Barnes & Noble bookseller chains are growing rapidly. He notes that these two big booksellers are talking about creating another "place" where customers can hang out in their larger, 25,000+-square-foot stores. From a business model perspective, it does not look very attractive. You have deeply entrenched competitors who are well funded to expand their brick-and-mortar environment. To enter the marketplace without a unique advantage would be difficult at best.

Add to that, there's the capital needed to get started in the bookselling business—capital for store expansion, inventory, employees. And so on. But if you create a business model that looks at book purchasing and delivery differently—say, by offering wider availability and a simpler ordering process through the Internet, as well as to-your-doorstep delivery by UPS/Fedex, then the whole business model shifts.

> *"The only thing worse than starting something*
> *and failing . . . is not starting something."*
> **—Seth Godin, author and marketer**

By shifting the manner in which people find out about and obtain their books, Jeff Bezos created a new kind of e-commerce platform. In time, he leveraged that access to customers to distribute multiple other products, not just books. In the process, he created something that traditional bookstores did not have: a strong database of customers who can then be cross-marketed and sold those other products. All with less overhead.

The only things that were initially different in Amazon.com's company design were its purchase and delivery strategy. Same books. Same customers. Same basic pricing. Different delivery. Purchases on the Internet can be made 24 hours a day, and subject-matter searches reveal all available books on a topic. Delivery follows rapidly upon order. Along with marketplace timing, reading trends, and listening to customers, Bezos created that powerful business model we know today as Amazon.com. Pretty good business model, great execution.

It seems simple. But remember that a great idea with a weak business model will ultimately fail. You need to refine and mold your business model so that it becomes a strategic weapon. Can your business model be as great as or better than your idea?

> *A great idea with a weak business*
> *model to sustain it will ultimately fail.*

But, getting back to the Osterwalder and Pigneur "canvas" mentioned in Chapter Two, one of the reasons it is so powerful is that it is so simple. The entire business model can be seen on a single sheet of paper and then modified on that same sheet of paper. (See the next section for more on the "canvas.") The other thing the business model canvas does is that it forces you to focus on the critical elements of your business model. Even if you are not a marketing expert, you need to see your business's "value proposition" from the customer's point of view, not your point of view. In other words, what makes your product or service unique so that a customer will care about it?

Many entrepreneurs are so "in love" with their idea that they don't see its potential flaws, whether those flaws are in their product, their strategy, or their business model. Yet, once I start walking them through the elements of the business model and I question their strategy, only then can they see the flaws. These are flaws, by the way, that can be corrected. It just takes more focus, more customer insight, perhaps investigating a distribution channel a little bit better, maybe developing a key partner relationship with a manufacturer. But it is at this point of realization that you really start to think in terms of developing a business, rather than starting a company. Big difference.

BUILD A REAL BUSINESS MODEL

A critical element of the LeanModel Framework is the early identification, iteration, and evolution of a start-up business model. It's the one question I ask almost anyone who approaches me with an idea for a new business opportunity. Rather than asking a general question about the business idea, I ask specific questions related to the business model. How is your product unique? Who is your target customer segment? What is your distribution strategy? Do you have multiple revenue streams? Quite a few entrepreneurs are not able to answer these critical questions in a detailed and confident manner.

"What constitutes a business model?" I asked the crowd at a start-up weekend event about four years ago. Not one of the college students and would-be entrepreneurs in attendance could articulate what a business model was or what its key elements are. That was pretty amazing. Despite everyone's talking about business models and acting like they know what it was, most people really haven't a clue.

Most experts will define what a business model is with a few variations, and most will agree on the key elements of a business model. Here is a generic description: *A business model is a design for the successful operation of a business, identifying revenue sources, customer base, products, and details of financing.*

The Business Model Building Blocks

No matter how you define a business model, it's the business model *elements* we are most interested in. These are the building blocks of the business, the essentials. Consider it a business blueprint. In their book *Business Model Generation*, Osterwalder and Pigneur devised a simple way for an entrepreneur to focus on and iterate his or her start-up business model. As I mentioned earlier, they created something they call the *business model canvas*. It's a useful tool (see Figure 3.1) for any entrepreneur, at any level. I have been using it in my entrepreneurship courses since 2011.

Undergraduate students in my classes easily understand the canvas, and within six weeks, they are creating a business model built around an idea, talking to about 75 customers, iterating the business model with what they learned, talking to another 50 customers, evolving or pivoting the business, then beginning to complete other areas of the business model, such as obtaining key partners and setting distribution strategies. By constantly updating their model with cus-

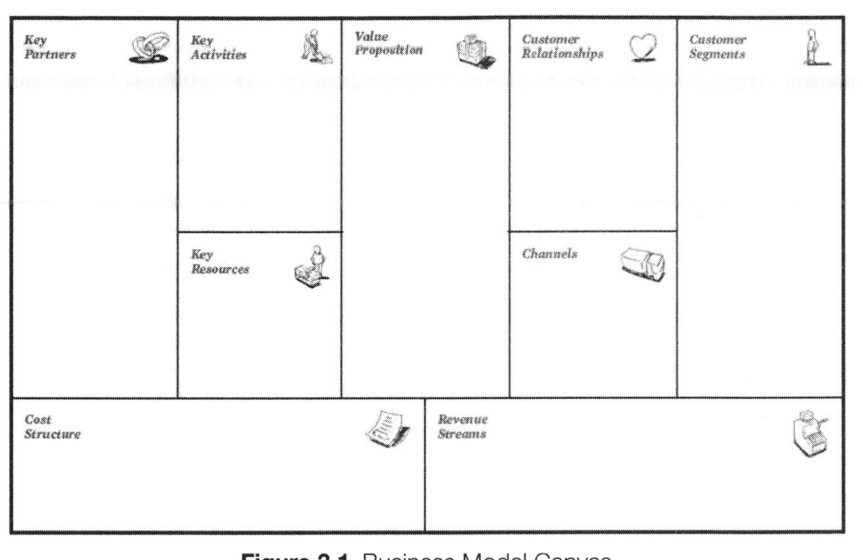

Figure 3.1 Business Model Canvas
(From *Business Model Generation*, ©2010 by Osterwalder and Pigneur.
Used with permission; www.businessmodelgeneration.com)

tomer feedback and input, at the end of 10 weeks they have a good idea of whether they are actually on to something or if they should abandon the idea.

You know what I like about seeing a group of students going through this process in a classroom? They rarely fall in love with an idea; instead, we vote on the best ideas in the class, then assign them randomly so their analysis and evolution of a business model is done somewhat objectively and honestly. They don't "fudge" the results to please an ego or creatively avoid reality, as could be done in forming some business plans.

Furthermore, they are not so in love with the idea that they are blind to its critical flaws. Based on their research and discussions with customers, potential partners, and distributors, if they cannot design a solid business model around the idea, they recommend abandonment. As it happens, student grades in these classes are based not on whether the students can create a successful business model, but on their recommendations of the business worthiness of those potential ideas. Love it.

The Key Components

If you are an entrepreneur or aspire to be one, here are the key elements of a business model, using the business model canvas just presented. Remember, as you investigate and gather feedback on each element of your business model, you will be making changes to that business model canvas. Get used to making changes—you will make a lot of them as your business model gets refined. But let's go into each element in detail and consider some starter questions. To review, here are the key elements of the business model.

- Unique Value Proposition

- Customer Relationship Feeling

- Customer Target Segments

- Distribution Channel Strategies

- Start-up Activities

- Start-up Resources

- Partners, Strategic and Tactical

- Product or Service Costs

- Selling/Revenue Sources

Now, let's consider each of these in turn.

THE UNIQUE VALUE PROPOSITION

The very core of a product or service idea is that it, in a unique and demonstrable way, solves a customer problem or delivers a customer solution. Most entrepreneurs struggle with this concept in regard to their idea. Instead of truly solving a customer problem, entrepreneurs potentially design a solution in search of either customers or problems. In fact, quite a few entrepreneurs feel they have to have an "epiphany" to come up with something unique. In reality, you would be better served looking at large marketplaces, understanding trends, and looking for customer problems.

IDEO is an amazing company that solves problems and creates potential products for Fortune 500 firms and well-heeled start-ups. If you look at their chart on market opportunity (see Figure 3.2), you will see that most product or service innovation opportunities come from iterations or evolutions of current or past products or services. Very few things are revolutionary.

The cellphone was revolutionary. Perhaps also the microwave oven. And for sure, the refrigerator. Yet today's household brands were not the revolutionaries. Google was not the first search engine. Facebook was not the first social media company. These companies offered incremental, or perhaps evolutionary, products. *And there's*

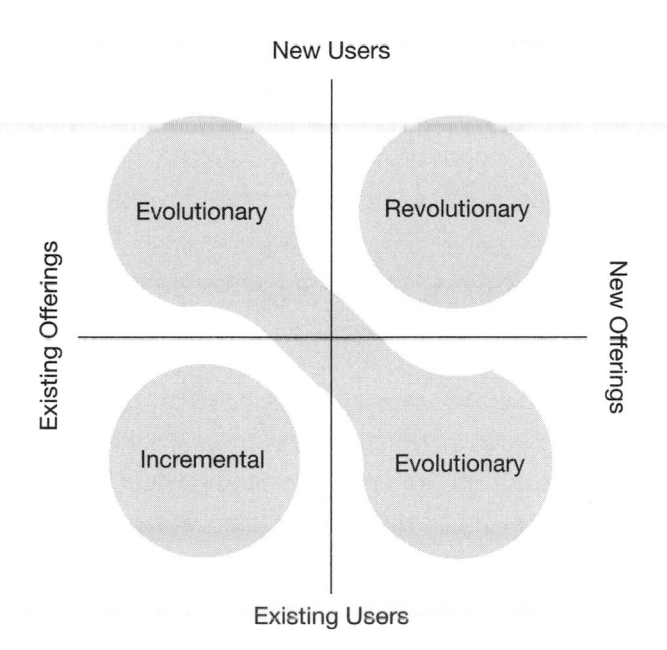

Figure 3.2 Startup Opporutunities for New Products or Services
(From IDEO.org, "Human-Centered Design Toolkit," used with permission)

nothing wrong with that. You can create quite a valuable company by listening to the marketplace and doing something just a little bit better, in your own, unique way.

As an entrepreneur, you have a choice. You can wait for an epiphany, you can design something you like or believe in (not sure if customers need it), or you can study marketplaces so hard that you will eventually learn about a customer problem. You can study and intersect trends à la Steve Jobs, and try to predict what customers will need. In any event, you validate the problem or opportunity and test a potential solution with real customers. If they react positively, you rapidly improve the prototype and test it again.

For instance, you try to add a unique element to an existing product or service that customers need and you can defend offering. If you can't deliver something unique, then get ready for the competitors. Books.com was the first bookseller on the Internet. That did not bother Amazon.com. The company proved their concept, focused on excellent customer service, accessed the largest number of books available through two distributors, and raised several million dollars to create a high level of brand awareness. They flew past the early entrants and quickly dominated the marketplace.

CUSTOMER RELATIONSHIP FEELING

There's a reason I linked the word *feeling* with the words *customer relationship.* While you can create marketing messages, creative advertising, or unique events, your real goal is to consider this: How do I create my product or service so well that customers actually "feel" an emotion when using my product or service? You can't make someone "feel" some way with your marketing. It has to come from within the customer. Really great companies and brands figure out a way to accomplish this goal. Let me give you an example.

Before 2008, Starbucks never advertised on television or print media, and then they began to do so only because of a weak stock price and some new competition from McDonald's. Everything customers experienced from the brand came from within the stores themselves and the staff. Greeting customers, knowing their names after a while, the warm store décor, even the unique flavor combinations of coffee. Customers would hang out there with friends or even alone, using services such as the wireless network, listening to the soft music playing. Seriously, it's just coffee. But they made most people *feel something* about being there. They even named it, calling it the "third place." Starbucks is an amazing example of a company's making people "feel" they deserved its product, that it was one of life's little pleasures.

Customers are not always right but they are never wrong.

Apple is another company that employs simplicity, beautiful design, and a great user interface to give customers products that are similar and yet uniquely different from the competition. This approach allows them to delight customers while charging them premium prices for those products. Safe to say, I *love* my iPhone.

Will your new product or service create an emotional feeling that distinguishes it from the competition? Are you a social entrepreneur, bringing a cause to the public's attention through sales? For example, Tom's Shoes is a nonprofit company that sends money and shoes from its sales to people all over the world through their One for One program. Do you think Tom's Shoes are unique? Or do you simply believe in their cause? It does not matter what you think, but it matters what Tom's customers think. And more important, it matters what they feel when they purchase Tom's products. It must be working because according to *Fast Company* magazine, Tom's revenue was estimated at more than $250 million in 2013.

As you consider your product or service, examine the customer relationship you want to build: what you want your customers to "feel" as they consume or use your product. If you are not sure what that feeling is, spend some time with potential customers. Find out what frustrates them about the current product or service they are using. Do you see an opportunity to create a solution that delights them? If so, you could potentially win big.

CUSTOMER TARGET SEGMENTS

Often when I meet with entrepreneurs and we end up talking about customers, I ask this question: Who is your niche target customer segment? Let's assume, for example, the product under consideration is intended for young women. So the entrepreneurs might reply, "It's for women ages 18 to 40." According to the U.S. Census of 2010, that would be approximately 90 million women. That's an entire market, not a target segment, let alone a niche segment.

Then, I ask the next question: Within that larger group, who are your early adopters or early influencers?" They might answer, "Oh, that would be women in college." That number now drops to approximately 11 million in the United States. Then I ask another question about women in college. You get the picture.

By the time we are done, we have identified perhaps a target group of less than 1 million women between the ages of 18 and 24, and perhaps a niche segment of less than 250,000 in a given regional market. It's not that you wouldn't eventually be able to sell to all the women in the entire market. You just need to focus, focus, focus in order to get serious traction with your first niche group of target customers. Then, as you conquer that group, you expand to the next segment, then the next segment, and that's how you move into the broader marketplace.

When we were working with Jeff Bezos of Amazon.com in those early days, we initially identified our first niche target customer among 1.3 million people living along the New York to Washington, D.C., corridor and in two cities in California—Los Angeles and San Francisco—who either read the major newspapers, bought a lot of books, or loved early technology. They were the influencers, the early adopters. So that's who we targeted with our initial marketing efforts.

The message is this: Make sure you know everything about your target segment of potential customers. Obtain demographic information (facts like age, sex, residency, etc.) and the psychographic details (lifestyle, interests, etc.). If you believe you have more than one customer segment, then determine if you need to treat the segment groups differently. For instance, would a product attribute have to be changed to fit one or the other group? Do the groups require different distribution strategies? Should there be multiple price points on the product? Focus first on the most important segment, then work additional segments, one at a time. It's too hard to handle multiple segments simultaneously and to juggle varying products or customer needs.

DISTRIBUTION CHANNEL STRATEGIES

Once you have a solid grasp of your unique value proposition and have identified your key target customer segments, you need to consider how you will get your product to the marketplace. If you consider entry into a marketplace from a number of "channels," evaluate the workings of direct sales, wholesalers, retailers, distributors, and selling online; of the latter, consider either your website or online retailers like eBay or Amazon.com. Each distribution channel provides different options for dealing with customers and prospects. The key question should always be: What is the best way to reach my initial target segment of customers? Or, simply, where do they want to buy the product or service?

You initially choose the distribution strategy that's best for your start-up based on whether you want to enter the marketplace quickly (more distribution, lower gross margin, higher potential sales) or slowly (direct sales, online sales, local retailers, higher gross margins).

Your distribution strategy may also be determined by the availability of your product. If it's a mobile application, there's no problem. If it's a physical product that needs to be manufactured, then you may be constrained by inventory or cash flow.

If your strategy is to grow your business regionally or nationally, you need to research geographical areas and the customers you want to reach through a distribution channel, then identify key distributors or retailers that provide coverage of those territories. If you are planning an export/import business, you focus on established distributors with demonstrated local market knowledge.

Consider also how you will market your products online so that you can extend coverage to customers where there is no suitable physical distribution network. In working with Dustin, a local entrepreneur who developed a healthy food product, we discovered that initially he thought about selling the product online and through local stores. But after just six months, Dustin's product was in only 20 stores. Once he started to investigate distribution networks by region, he began concentrating on selling to key distributors and retailers (regional retail brands with more than 25 locations). In the next six months, Dustin added 500 store locations by closing deals with two key distributors and four regional brands. He gave up some product gross margin but got tremendous sales volume in exchange.

Would you rather make $15,000 on sales of $100,000 (15 percent profit) or $150,000 on sales of $1 million (also 15 percent profit) through distributors/retail chains? Product sales volume solves a lot of cash-flow problems. You will always need more cash to fund additional inventory. These are the considerations that determine the distribution decisions you make.

I mentor Adam, an entrepreneur who does about $3 million a year in revenue exclusively through Amazon.com. He sells more than 100 different products based on observing customer trends. He also gives up some fees (gross margin) selling on that online platform. I asked him why he doesn't build his own website, search-engine optimize it, and sell directly to his customers. Adam responded, "Amazon.com has over 235 million customer credit cards on file. . . they are like a huge mall, and I want to be in that mall. Besides, at my volume, they also fulfill and ship all my products so I don't need a warehouse." Adam runs the entire business out of his condo. That's a LeanModel Framework business.

As you consider your options, your distribution strategy should take account of the potential revenue and gross margin contribution of each distribution channel. Good distributors also provide you with local market insight and other customer bases, enabling you to establish your business in new regions without incurring additional marketing and sales costs. Before you make any distribution decisions, though, talk to some local retailers who have distribution experience or consider meeting with the distributors to better understand their services and operations. Since this area is so critical to the business model, thorough research is required.

START-UP ACTIVITIES

This is an area that can simply be overwhelming to a beginning entrepreneur. It can seem like you have everything to do and not enough time to do it. Here is some advice. Let your current business model help you focus on what really needs to be done regarding the launch of the business.

I know entrepreneurs who agonize about the myriad things that have to be done, to the point they become overwhelmed or even paralyzed. Slow down. If you examine your business model carefully, you can prioritize based on what needs to be done to rapidly build a prototype of your product or service. Look at each of the business model segments and identify the critical elements that require research or a solution. For instance:

- Do I need to learn more about my target customer segments?

- Do I need to define a minimum viable product specification?

- Do I know enough to determine my distribution strategy?

- Have I found a manufacturer for my product?

- Do I need a business location or will I be a virtual business?

- Who else do I need to meet to refine my overall business strategy?

- Am I aware of key trends in my proposed marketplace?

- How can I quickly get a prototype of my product or service built?

Keep referring to your business model and look for the gaps or the unknowns that keep you from quickly building a prototype. That should drive your key activities.

START-UP RESOURCES

If you have done a reasonably good job of focusing on key start-up activities, that action will identify the resources you will need to launch your product. Foremost, of course, might be the need for capital. Okay, you will always need more money than you think you will need.

Review your proposed product or service for whether it is appropriate for crowdfunding or an equity project on a crowdfunding platform. Review other projects currently on KickStarter, IndieGogo, and other crowdfunding websites; determine your possibility of raising funds or distributing equity to raise the funds that will support your start-up business.

In terms of the product or service you are looking to rapidly prototype, determine what resources you will need to actually build it. Will you try to build it in-house or will you outsource the product development? Consider keeping your company as "virtual" as possible.

Resist the urge to do things that accumulate additional expenses, like taking office space or acquiring the trappings of a traditional business.

I mentor an entrepreneur duo who launched their company with friends and family money of $30,000 (borrowed and paid back) to support one kiosk location in 2011 while they were still on campus as undergraduates. They now have six locations and will do more than $2 million in revenue in 2014. They still don't have an office (they meet on campus, in our center or at Starbucks, with their key employees), they still drive older cars, and they still live in a house with three other people. I keep advising them to put every possible dollar back into the business to open more locations. They have followed a LeanModel Framework strategy and own 100 percent of their company's equity.

The other key resource you will need is people. For example, do you need someone to program or build something? If so, refrain from giving people equity unless they are mission-critical. And if that's the case, let them earn the equity over two to three years. If they aren't critical to your success, work out a deferred compensation arrangement instead of equity.

Similarly, you can raise capital through friends and family or crowdfunding to pay for having your prototype developed. Don't throw equity around in those early days. There are a couple of reasons. For one, you will need that equity down the road for attracting really critical partners or key hires. And, two, I have seen more entrepreneurs in court or arbitration hearings due to a break-up or difference in strategy. That usually occurs in the early stages of a company, and it's often a fight over mythical equity value. That is, the equity really isn't worth anything yet, as the start-up is either pre-revenue or is operating at a loss. And these disputes usually happen when the parties don't really know each other well, don't trust each other, or don't accept each other's strengths and weaknesses. A sign of true equity partnership is when the parties share a passion to create the company—that outweighs everything else.

PARTNERS, STRATEGIC AND TACTICAL

As you refine your business model and evaluate how to produce your product or get your product into the marketplace, you begin to identify key partners who can help you accomplish your objectives.

Trust yourself. Trust your instinct. And if you are
going to build a company, learn how to trust others.

Partners, by the way, can be both tactical and strategic. You should treat both with the same amount of respect. Never make someone feel he or she is "just" a vendor to you; make everyone you deal with like you and like your start-up mission so much that they want to help you.

Although there are any number of partner types, let's look at three key areas:

- *Manufacturers:* This could be an outsourced team of people, freelancers, or actual manufacturers who could design and produce your product prototype.

- *Distributors:* These would be key distribution channel partners who will help you take your product to various marketplaces.

- *Suppliers:* These would be key suppliers or vendors who are supplying you with your product components necessary to produce your final product.

Before you choose any of these partners, talk to other entrepreneurs who have gone down a similar path. They have gained experience and knowledge that you need. They have also done some things right and have made some mistakes. You want to learn from them so that you don't make the same mistakes.

Depending on the industry you are in, find out who the key manufacturers and suppliers are. If you have time, attend a trade show for manufacturers where you will learn even more.

When you do choose a key partner, move slowly, if you can. Get to know each other. If you are building a product, agree on the specifications of the product in writing. Don't order a large quantity; order in small batches until you are satisfied the product is being built correctly.

In talking to quite a few entrepreneurs, I have heard the same story over and over again. *We were moving too quick. We assumed they knew what they were doing. We ordered 3,000 instead of a first batch of 300 products.* All agreed they had sacrificed quality for speed or cost savings. All agreed they made a mistake. It's okay to move fast, but you cannot sacrifice product quality. No matter what your brand promise is, or how great everything looks, if the quality is not exceptional, you are in real trouble.

PRODUCT OR SERVICE COSTS

You will have some start-up costs as you conduct research and look to eventually build a prototype of your product or service. In terms of the business model, focus on the actual product or service ongoing costs, or the cost for each product at some level of volume.

You need to build your assumptions for your product costs, so set up a spreadsheet and identify all the costs related to the product itself. Let's call these *direct costs* (like direct materials, direct labor, and manufacturing expenses). Then, let's add all the *indirect costs*—those not related to the product itself (like marketing, travel expenses, rent, and labor other than direct labor).

Once you have a handle on estimating your expenses, move everything into a 12-month forecast sheet and estimate, conservatively, your projected revenues and expenses from month 1 through month 12. Based on this forecast sheet, you can tell if you are actually making money (are you profitable each month?). But, more importantly, you can tell how much money you need on hand *before* you start your company.

This *before* money is needed to fund the initial inventory and sales expenses. Plan on having enough money to fund the next inventory shipment, as you will still be receiving funds in staggering amounts from distributors or customers. If your product is online software, you may be cash-flow positive right from the start of the company.

But it's not enough to fund just the next manufacturing order. You also have to determine how much money you need on hand, via yourself, friends, and family or perhaps by raising funds via a crowd-funding platform. Don't be naïve about how much cash you need. Quite a few entrepreneurs have launched their companies without enough cash on hand to fund inventory replenishment or critical product refinement. As a consequence, the young businesses struggled or even failed. They failed not because the products were not good, but because the entrepreneurs simply ran out of cash. In the early days of a start-up, *cash flow is king*. Never forget that.

SELLING/REVENUE SOURCES

It's important that you step back and identify all the potential revenue sources for your product or service. Initially, you may see only one or two potential revenue sources. But there are usually more.

While you don't have to pursue these possibilities all at once, from a strategic perspective you do need to be aware of them and of their potential. To help you with this, here are two examples using real companies.

Manufactured Retail Fashion Product

Jenny wanted to create a company that would help others via an important social cause. She purposely wanted to create a triple-bottom company (people, profit, and planet). She selected a fashion product to launch her start-up for which a certain portion of the net profit would fund her cause. Jenny assumed she would be selling online using her own website and also in local retail stores. After being in business for one year, here are the potential revenue sources she has identified:

- Own Website

- Local Retail Stores

- Regional Brand Stores

- National Brand Stores

- Other Websites

- Private Label

- Licensing to Other Brands Overseas

Now that she has a bigger picture of potential revenue sources, she can make both tactical and strategic decisions that will grow her company.

Software Products

Dmitri noticed a popular e-commerce platform had achieved more than 20 million downloads. As he investigated the platform, he became frustrated by a few user-centric problems. So he created some simple software tools and widgets for the platform. He started by selling them on his website to developers and sophisticated customers. But as he investigated the marketplace for this platform, and the e-commerce marketplace in general, he discovered he had more options. So in year two, Dmitri began to utilize multiple revenue opportunities:

- Own Website

- E-Commerce Platform Website

- Several "Influencer" Developer Websites

- Portal Website for Developer Tools
- Key Product Partners via Bundling

Understanding the complete marketplace allowed him to utilize several revenue opportunities, which have resulted in a quintupling of his annual revenue.

* * *

The key is to examine the marketplace and understand how and where customers want to purchase your product or service. After reviewing every possible revenue opportunity, then you decide, perhaps in the order of priority, which revenue streams to initially pursue, knowing you can add others eventually.

Selling. There was a reason I titled this section "Selling/Revenue Sources." You are not going to drive any revenue unless you know how to *sell* your product or service. If you have never had any experience selling, then talk with people who are comfortable selling, attend a seminar on selling, and take a part-time job selling something.

***As an entrepreneur, you are either going
to sell something or not. It's up to you.***

You need to be comfortable with the job of selling; in fact, your sales skills are what will drive your company forward. Most entrepreneurs think they can just launch their company and the sales will magically appear. *That won't happen.* So if you believe you will never be good at selling your company's products or services, then find a partner or co-founder who thrives on selling. Also, read *Spin Selling* by Neil Rackham. It really helped me understand the complete sales process, the three key customer types, why people buy (want versus need), and how, if done right, they will actually buy from you as opposed to you constantly thinking you need to sell them something. And you can't really sell something unless you have the answers to some important questions related to your business model.

A well-designed business model is a critical element of the Lean-Model Framework. Instead of writing a "perfect" business plan, you develop, integrate, and evolve a solid business model. Here is the summary of questions you should know or be able to answer regarding your business model. They are listed by the various elements of the business model and are not intended to be a definitive list, just thought starters.

Unique Value Proposition

- What value will my product or service deliver to the customer?

- Which customer problem am I solving?

- Am I satisfying a customer need?

- What is the minimum viable product?

- Is my product offering unique and defensible?

Customer Relationship Feeling

- What kind of relationship do I want with my customers?

- What do I want them to say or feel about my product or service?

- How costly is it to build a relationship?

- Can I create the relationship I want in my business model?

Customer Target Segments

- What is the size of the marketplace?

- Is the marketplace growing or changing?

- Who is my initial target segment?

- Who is my secondary target segment?

- What are unique characteristics of each segment?

- Do I have to communicate or reach those segments in different ways?

Distribution Channel Strategies

- What distribution channels should I consider?

- Where are my customers?

- How do competitors reach their customers now?

- Are there new trends that will affect distribution channels?

- Which are different distribution channel pros and cons?

- Is this a new or growing customer segment?

Start-Up Activities

- What are key things I need to do now?

- Have I investigated various distribution strategies?

- Have I investigated various revenue streams?

- How could I create a minimum viable product?

- How and where should I incorporate?

Start-up Resources

- What key resources do I need to get started?

- What resources do I need for distribution, customer relationship, and to create revenue?

- What can I outsource?

- What do I need in-house?

- Do I have the talent I need?

- Should I create a crowdfunding campaign?

Partners, Strategic and Tactical

- Who are tactical partners/suppliers?

- Who are strategic partners?

- What key resources will I get from partners?

- What key activities do partners support?

- Who are my competitors working with?

Product or Service Costs

- What is the current cost of a product or service similar to mine?

- What will it cost me to produce the product or service?

- How can I outsource or cut my costs?

- At what point will product or service costs go down based on volume?

Selling/Revenue Sources

- What do current customers pay for a product or service like mine?

- What would I expect my customers to pay?

- What are the potential revenue streams (retail, online, licensing, etc.)?

- Will my revenue produce a gross margin or profit to sustain my business model?

ENTREPRENEUR INSIGHT

About three years ago, I was approached by an entrepreneur who had spotted an opportunity in the marketplace of social media tools. He had done a significant amount of research, had met with several technologists, even met with a few angel investors. At the time we had our conversation, I noted that he might only have a short "marketplace window" in which to launch his product and that he needed to get going. He indicated that, based on feedback from potential investors, he was going to take the time to craft a business plan. I told him to develop a prototype quickly and to move faster.

He spent six months developing a business plan and began to pitch investors. They told him they needed to see "traffic" and a proof of concept. He spent another nine months taking too much time to build the "perfect" prototype. He launched the prototype into the marketplace. Too late. Another company had already launched the same product.

KEY TAKEAWAY

The LeanModel Framework has four different and important interlinked components. But speed to market is critical. Build a solid business model. Use lean resources. Test your prototype. Get customer feedback. Move faster.

CHAPTER FOUR

Lean Resources: Less Is More

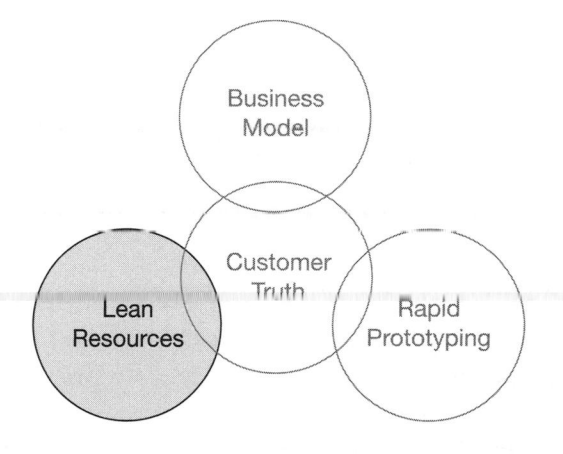

There are several definitions of the word *entrepreneur*. I like this one, by Stevenson, the best: "[T]he pursuit of opportunity without regard to resources currently controlled." In other words, you run forward even though you don't have all the resources at present to build the product or service. You just keep moving forward, knowing that at some point you will figure it out. But there is good news. There has never been a better time to employ a "lean resources" mentality, as there are so many lean resources that can help you. Let me explain.

In past experience at various companies, I managed annual budgets ranging from $25,000 to over $100 million. If you think that having more money yields better creativity, guess again. Do you know when our teams were most creative? When we had small budgets— or almost no budgets. People tend to think more creatively when they have to get around a lack of funds or resources. What I discovered over time is that, in order to be successful, it's best to adopt a lean resources mentality.

> *"Genius is one percent inspiration and*
> *ninety-nine percent perspiration."*
> —**Thomas Edison,** *Life*

More often than not, it's the mentality or behavior of an entrepreneur that attracts people and resources; they just come up with creative solutions. Don't have the money for public relations? Create such a powerful story or event that it is written about in the local or national press. Don't have money for a trade show booth? Attend the event with samples or images of your product and look for buyers anyway. Can't pay to have your food product sampled at a retail location? Get a table at a farmers' market and sell your product there. Need additional capital or a way to generate pre-sales? Create a crowdfunding campaign.

LEAN RESOURCES ARE EVERYWHERE

In today's business world, technology and new emerging marketplaces allow an entrepreneur to accomplish an incredible amount with lean resources. For instance, you can use cloud Software as a Service (SaaS) tools to build your own website, virtually for free. You can source small amounts of your product and sell them on Amazon.com to test the idea and generate some revenue at the same time. You can take that amazing pulled pork barbeque recipe and sell pulled pork tacos at a farmers' market as a test for starting a food truck. The new 3D printers allow you to create prototypes for very little money. You can build a mobile application in your spare time, test it with friends, refine it, and put it up for sale in an online app store. Additionally, social networks have become so powerful that, for little money, you can craft an online marketing campaign to drive product awareness and sales.

How many more food-truck success stories do we need to hear? They are a great way to test a new food concept, at a significantly lower cost than opening a restaurant. Let's see. . . . What are the average U.S. national costs to start a new "food concept" restaurant? $500,000. What are the average costs to start a food-truck business? $50,000 or less.

Many businesses can be started simply with a little capital. If you are an accountant, tax attorney, marketing expert, chef, painter, car detailer, and the like, start a consulting practice or weekend business to test your idea. Love dogs? Open a dog-sitting or dog-walking business in an urban area. A small lifestyle business can give you the pleasure and income you desire, or it can grow into a large company. So, start something you care about.

Look, it's takes lots of hard work to make your new business successful. It just does not have to take lots of money. It will, however, require having a lean resources mentality. In early January 2011, two students indicated they would like to participate in our annual Entrepreneur Day, held on the campus every March. I asked them what they planned on selling. Sunglasses. But they did not have them yet. They had no idea how long it would take to get them manufactured. We agreed they should go offshore, get some stylish sunglasses in the university colors, and sell them at a price point they could test. With customer feedback, they could take a little more time and have a line of sunglasses created for them. They ordered 300 sunglasses at $3 each and sold them all for $20 each. They took those profits, created a crowdfunding IndieGogo campaign to raise even more funds, and designed their own sunglasses brand. Today, they have sales of over $750,000 with their unique line of sunglasses selling in six countries.

BUILD A COMPANY TO FUND A COMPANY

I have been mentoring an entrepreneur who is using the most amazing strategy to generate revenue in an existing "commodity products" business—all to fund his next big idea when it arrives. Over the past six years, and starting with a $3,000 credit card purchase for some HDMI cables from China, Adam has grown his online e-commerce business to over $3 million per year. He sells more than 100 different products, with an average gross margin of 60 percent.

Adam has become an online e-commerce expert, is highly experienced in search-engine optimization, and is insanely curious about products and trends. He is always selling products that I just heard about, so there is always growing customer demand for a good period of time, usually about 24 months. He does not even have his own website. Adam sells everything on other online platforms and outsources the operations and shipping as well. He runs the entire business out of his condominium, and uses university student interns to assist him. Talk about running a LeanModel Framework business!

But Adam has created this business over time to do two things: First, to provide him with an entrepreneurial lifestyle; and second, to generate enough cash flow so that he can fund a big idea when he sees one. Well, he sees one now and has the cash on hand to set up the business, test a prototype, and see if he is on to something. Whatever his result, it's an amazing fundraising strategy that builds one business to fund another. And Adam will hold 100 percent equity in both companies. Consider if this strategy makes sense for you.

LEVERAGE IS KEY

As an entrepreneur, you use that LeanModel Framework mentality in order to move faster to take advantage of an opportunity. As part of that philosophy, you need to leverage all the lean resources that are available to you. Even if you have raised the necessary capital to fund a new opportunity, you want to extend your "runway" of cash as far as you can. The traditional term for how you go through cash on hand via time is called the *burn rate*. That is, how many months of cash do you have to launch and run your company?

That is the traditional view. However, I propose that you launch and run your new start-up so lean that you might actually produce cash early on to help fund the company. How about creating a rapid *earn rate* mentality that produces revenue as fast as possible? Another strategy is to keep your expenses extremely low. You need to leverage everything.

Let's walk through the major areas that you should be aware of regarding resources that you can leverage:

- People Are Experts, Too

- Local and Global Talent

- Local Community

- Financing Options

- Technology Tools

- Manufacturing

PEOPLE ARE EXPERTS, TOO

When students ask me what the most important thing is that they can acquire while they are in school, and for a few years after they graduate, I have a two-word answer: skill sets. As a person looking to shape a career, and potentially become an entrepreneur, you have to build and strengthen your skill sets to the point where you can potentially be an expert in your given area.

Being an expert gives you several options. One option is to leverage your expertise into creating a company by treating yourself as a "rapid prototype." That is, you use your talents and expertise to launch a company around an expertise you already possess. For example, I am mentoring several entrepreneurs who started their companies on a part-time or weekend basis. In a short time, or over a few years, they have become experts in a given area, where they can leverage that expertise to start a company. Some examples:

- Online marketing expert in either search-engine optimization or social-media marketing

- Forensic accounting specialist who understands how to do a solid financial analysis

- Sustainability or environmental specialist who advises other companies

- Photography expert who creates several businesses including online photography classes

Examine your skill set and determine if you can launch a potential company around that expertise you have, and then add more services or products once you get traction in the marketplace.

LOCAL AND GLOBAL TALENT

Leverage the expertise or work abilities of others around you, either in your local community or worldwide, using Internet technology. I assume you are aware of the workforce resources in your local marketplace. Utilize that network to leverage any resources that might be available at local universities.

For example, at our Lavin Entrepreneurship Center, we annually place more than 50 student interns in positions with small companies in the area. We have other resources on the campus, including student incubators and specialty courses in engineering, science, and mobile computing where, as part of their graduation requirements, students have to create a product. Most universities have similar course requirements that involve practical applications, and you can leverage these resources for your own product development. The potential at local universities is underutilized; if I were creating a company today, I would locate it two blocks from a major university.

> *If I were creating a company today, I would*
> *locate it two blocks from a major university.*

Other great local resources are community incubators, small business centers, co-location facilities, start-up programs, start-up weekends, and shared community resources. Often, local business organizations offer free services or even a small office to help young companies get started. In addition to accessing these resources, you'll be spending time with other people looking to create companies; you'll network your way into local entrepreneur groups. Indeed, what you could learn and leverage from other local entrepreneurs might be immeasurable in its value to your start-up.

I mentor an entrepreneur who developed some software tools. We realized Andrew might be better able to grow his company by placing him in a technical, entrepreneurial environment and still keep his company costs low. He moved to San Francisco, took a co-location office inside of RocketSpace (a start-up company co-location facility), leveraged the 50+ other technology-oriented entrepreneurs inside that facility, and leveraged four software freelance contractors located in four different countries; the result was that Andrew tripled the revenue of his company, all with just one employee—himself.

As you craft your business model and do your research on your opportunity, evaluate the resources of elance (www.elance.com) and oDesk (www.odesk.com). These are just two of several online communities that can provide a pool of freelance talent to help you out in a variety of ways. For instance, you can place "projects" on these websites and have people bid on them. Then, if you select someone to do the work and it's done correctly, you accept the work and pay the individual.

While this method accesses an immense pool of potential talent, do your due diligence before hiring anyone. For example, ask for references and descriptions of past projects completed. While the advantage of a freelance market is its worldwide talent pool, a disadvantage is its potential complications of different time zones and cultural attitudes. You can use online tools like file sharing and video conferencing to handle the communications, which speeds delivery.

LOCAL COMMUNITY

More often than not, I find that entrepreneurs don't know much about all the critical resources available in their local communities. It's essential you know the resources available locally. Aside from the nearby talent described earlier, resources could include other entrepreneurs, potential mentors, co-location facilities, incubators, "free" or shared space inside another company, and city or state grant-sponsored facilities or programs.

In addition, consider exploring the local "retail" opportunities to test your product or service, whether those are the local farmers' market, flea market, independent fashion goods store, organic food store, or local pet shop. If you think about who might help you get your product or service off the ground, and possibly assist in testing the waters, it will most likely be someone at the local level. Often they are entrepreneurs themselves and they will want to see you succeed.

If you test your product or service in such a local environment, be sure you have some measure of control in the supply, delivery, and selling processes. In others words, you test locally before you meet that national or global opportunity. The adage "You only get one chance to make a first impression" applies to entrepreneurial endeavors as well. It's easy to improve the product after it's been tested locally, but it's hard to recover when you have failed on the national stage.

Let's consider this entrepreneur: Isabelle started her company on the campus of her university when she was a student, and I managed to help her get the product placed in the university bookstore. At first, everything was great and her product was selling well, but then she started having quality problems. She quickly pulled the product, corrected the quality issues, and relaunched. Sales took off, and Isabelle slowly expanded into the local community, using independent retailers. She then expanded her store presence throughout the region and ultimately on a national level. Today, she has over 60 stores across the country carrying her products, and she is in discussion with two major retail brands, which would expand her distribution to over 200 stores. Why are those two brands interested in working with her? Because of the rave reviews she received in those 60 independent stores that carried her products.

FINANCING OPTIONS

Once you have crafted a solid business model around a real opportunity, and you have utilized the lean resources offered in your local and global community, you may need to identify ways to raise additional capital to fund the start-up. My hope is that you are doing something so lean that your start-up does not require a significant amount of cash. However, let's assume that you need a certain amount of capital to start the business and that you do not have that capital today.

First Stop: You

The first place to look for money is *you*. What can you downsize, sell, or eliminate to free up some cash? If you really believe in your opportunity, what skin are you willing to put in the game? Investors and venture capitalists love an entrepreneur who has invested in his or her own business, who has put down cash, made sacrifices, and contributed sweat equity. Investors invest in passionate people who have bet on themselves.

Banks or local lending facilities might also be an option. Find out if there are any city or state grants available for entrepreneurs. In addition, review your credit cards and their corresponding interest rates to see if that is a viable option. Remember, never risk more than you can afford to lose.

Friends and Family, Do it Right

I am always a bit nervous about recommending the use of friends and family as investors in your start-up business. For best results, don't treat them like investors—treat them like a friendly bank. Here are some simple but important rules that may help to keep your friendships and family intact:

- *Set expectations accordingly.* Even if you firmly believe that your start-up will be a success, it's smart to remind friends and family of the historical facts related to new businesses. More than 50 percent fail in the first two years, and even the "overnight successes" take five years to reach potential, on the average. This is not an investment strategy that makes sense. So ask them not to treat it like an investment.

- *It has to be their discretionary funds.* If friends and family are still willing to take the risk because they believe in you, you need to be convinced that they can afford to lose it all, without a major impact on their lives. If you are not sure on this matter, don't take their money.

- *It's a professional transaction.* Treat the transaction as you would expect to be treated by a bank. That means writing down and signing the terms of the agreement, after making sure everyone understands them. Insist on paying market rates for commercial loans, since the Internal Revenue Service has some specific rules related to gifts.

- *Repayments tied to your cash flow.* Since you don't really know when you will generate cash flow, try to avoid obligations with fixed repayment schedules. With cash flow obligations, investors receive a percentage of your operating cash flow (if any) until they have been repaid in full.

- *Loans are better than equity.* Offering debt is better than offering equity, especially in the early stages when you have no valuation for setting equity percentages. Plus, you don't want investors, especially friends and family, who really don't know your business questioning your every move.

- *Pay the money back quickly, wisely.* This loan is real and it needs to be paid back. However, some founders are too focused on quick repayment, and they compromise strategic decisions. Better to pay it back in smaller, consistent micro-payments unless your cash flow increases dramatically. If that's the case, pay it back.

TECHNOLOGY TOOLS

The technology available today is absolutely amazing. It's leveled the playing field for entrepreneurs looking to create a business, and it has enabled anyone to sell *something* to *someone, somewhere*. That's incredible, actually.

If you are looking to create a business, or you are already an entrepreneur, you have to be insane not to investigate the variety of technological tools at hand to start and manage your company. Even if you don't like technology, you need to understand the technology that might give you a competitive advantage.

For example, you might be selling organic honey from Australia, with special antioxidant properties. People all over the world might be looking for that honey. So, instead of just selling it in your local town in Australia, you utilize online marketing to drive sales on your website, or you can sell your products on Amazon.com and reach a global "online mall." In addition, several niche websites that focus on organic foods may want to sell your product. Thus, you can dramatically increase the chances for your success if you learn to utilize and leverage technology that is at extremely reasonable costs. Additionally, technology can help you keep your costs down and your opportunity high, which is critical to a start-up.

About two years ago, I helped a couple of student entrepreneurs start their business here on campus. They had created a healthy protein drink; think of it as a protein-based meal replacement, with fresh, natural ingredients, a simple menu with great pricing. Instead of putting them in a traditional brick-and-mortar environment, we convinced the university that everyone would be better served if they were located just outside the recreation center on campus, in a 20-by-10-foot stainless steel and black canvas kiosk. That recommendation meant not very much overhead—just electricity and water.

The business was so successful, the students now have six locations in California. They heavily utilize technology to run their business, though. The iPad touch screens serve as cash registers; a cloud-based point-of-sales system runs the business operation, including the financials, for $35 a month. They utilize Square (a wireless payments vendor) as their virtual merchant vendor to process customer payments. Also, they can "look into" the business from anywhere in the world via their smartphones, and "see" sales happening in real time, either in total or by location.

Instead of creating training manuals for the employees, these entrepreneurs developed training videos and posted them in a private YouTube account for managers and employees to access. What's more, this multi-million-dollar business does not have a corporate office. They conduct their meetings with employees and managers using local meeting places. Technology enables a lean resource mentality.

Specifically, there are two major groups of technological tools to consider. The first is what I call *technology platform tools*. These tools allow you to open a business and sell your product. The second, *technology-enabling tools*, allow you to market and run your business. As you could probably imagine, however, there are many more tools out there. Get curious.

Technology Platform Tools

With these technology tools you can either create or leverage existing Web technology platforms. On the creation side, there are simple but powerful website creation tools like WordPress, Weebly, Tumblr, and SquareSpace. These website-building tools, often free for a simple version or free for a trial period, allow you to rapidly build your website and begin showcasing your brand to the world. The advice here is to investigate all your options, and work with a freelance designer to create a powerful and useful website using one of these or several other website tools. The reason you want to use a website platform tool is for its ability to maintain and update your website without needing a programmer.

The next level of website platform tools especially designed for e-commerce are Shopify, Volusion, and Big Commerce. One of the entrepreneurs I mentor built his website using the Shopify e-commerce platform. He built his website in less than two weeks. The tool has a built-in editing feature, the ability to add and edit products, and several merchant choices that allow customers to use their credit cards for payment. The monthly website fees start at $28 per month. I am not endorsing Shopify; I just offer it to illustrate how these tools are used.

Another e-commerce tool is Big Commerce. About a year ago, we helped Mark, a local entrepreneur, to build his online e-commerce strategy. We chose Big Commerce, mostly for its robust capabilities. It has almost Amazon.com capabilities and features: built-in content editing, flexible shopping-cart options, easy export of all transactions to a financial tool like Quick Books, email capabilities, and more. All this comes with pricing that starts at less than $30 per month. We designed the website using Big Commerce themes and template pages—no programmer necessary—in less than two weeks, with multiple product categories and multiple products.

Technology-Enabling Tools

There are so many of these cloud-based tools that I don't know where to start. Here's a simple list of potential tools in the order you might use them when starting a company:

- LinkedIn: To build your network of knowledge experts, entrepreneurs, and industry experts

- Google Alerts: To bring you information on key subject matter via email

- Google Trends: To help you track online search trends

- Survey Monkey: To use for online potential customer surveys

- LegalZoom: To help you with your legal needs

- DropBox: To share files and collaborate with others

- Skype: To conduct face-to-face video meetings with employees and partners

- Square: To turn your smartphone or iPad into a cash register

- Constant Contact: To email prospects and customers

- HootSuite: To manage all your social-media marketing efforts from one platform

- POS Lavu: To keep track of point-of-sale and manage inventory

- YouTube: To post your product or demo videos online and on your website

- Google Analytics: To understand visitor traffic to your website

I don't know if there has ever been a time when so many tools were available to potential entrepreneurs. Anyone with access to the Internet can leverage these tools to support a start-up business. And quite a few of them are free, so take the time to learn the potential here—it could impact your new business in a big way.

MANUFACTURING

We had years during which industries moved their manufacturing overseas. It seemed that everyone who wanted to manufacture something would run to China. Cheaper labor. Cheaper costs. Now, manufacturing in the United States seems to be making a comeback. In several recent articles, experts cite the increase in "Made in the USA" advantages, which include reduced shipping expenses, more rapid turnaround of product design changes, and better quality control. The good news is that today's entrepreneurs have many options when considering who and where their product will be manufactured.

The first option is local manufacturing or distribution. Although the cost might be higher initially (owing to lower volumes or higher labor costs), the advantages of having your manufacturing and/or distribution partners available nearby are great. You can meet with people face to face—there's no substitute for that. You can visit the facility and truly understand its capabilities. You can be nearby as they build your prototype, allowing you to manage the process better. You can more easily review the product quality. In short, you save time and money by being close to each other. Obviously, the logistics of getting your product delivered to you or to stores in your local market are simplified with lower costs. So, examine your local marketplace first to determine if manufacturing nearby is a viable option.

When local isn't the best choice, China is still a strong source for manufacturing. I asked Adam, a local entrepreneur in San Diego, who sells more than 100 products and uses 10 manufacturers in China, what he would recommend to a novice entrepreneur looking to manufacture a product for the first time. Adam travels to China regularly and meets with several manufacturers each visit, usually at trade show events. Here are Adam's recommendations in regard to Chinese manufacturing:

1. Start by looking up the website www.alibaba.com and reviewing the kinds of products and pricing costs that are available
   from Chinese manufacturers. While you should not really select a manufacturer directly from this website without refer-
   rals or a recommendation, it will give you a great idea of
   what's possible.

2. Go to www.globalsources.com to get a better understanding
   of all the trade shows that are happening in that part of the
   world where manufacturers attend and show off their latest
   products and capabilities. You may find it worth your while
   to attend a specific trade show that may have 100 manufacturers showcasing a certain type of product or technology.

3. If you really want to "blow your mind," attend the Canton
   Fair in Guangzhou, where over 150,000 products are showcased and you can have face-to-face meetings with manufacturers to explore other products.

Here's one final comment, this on near-shore manufacturing:
Keep your eye on Mexico. The country is making solid strides with
cross-border programs and their manufacturing capabilities. Brad and
James are two local serial entrepreneurs, Brad in technology electron-
ics production, and James in fashion accessories and clothing. They
both utilize manufacturers in Mexico and they speak highly of the
quality, the reasonable costs, and the ability to ship to the United
States very quickly. Both Brad and James say they will increase their
business in Mexico versus China in the near future.

3D Printing Is the Local Wild Card

Keep your eye on 3D printing, as it will provide some interesting solutions for low-volume, unique products or prototypes. According to
Gartner Research, an industry analyst, 3D printing as an industry is
estimated to grow from more than $450 million in 2013 to over $5.7
billion in 2017. That's pretty rapid growth.

My predictions are that 3D printing will present some real entrepreneurial opportunities. First, we will see produced some specific, low-volume products made from 3D printers. For example, do you want to buy 100 customized smartphone cases as a giveaway at an event? You will be able to upload an image online, send it to your local store, where it will be printed to order, for your easy pickup. Or, do you like a special kitchen drawer knob, but need only 20 of them? No problem; the local home supply company will make them in-house with their 3D printer.

The entrepreneurial opportunities will increase incrementally as customers learn to design or create their own 3D-manufacturable products. Similarly, an entrepreneur can utilize 3D printing to rapidly prototype a product. Either way, you should learn about and keep your eye on 3D printing as either a service or an opportunity.

ENTREPRENEUR INSIGHT

About four years ago, Paul and Griffin, two college students, saved enough money to do one final surfing trip to Costa Rica after graduating. Then, as they told their parents, they would go out and get real jobs. But while on that trip, they noticed a wrist bracelet being sold on the beach. They each bought one. They liked them a lot, so they went back and bought 1,000 more with their remaining money. Once back on the mainland, they sold them to their friends—all of them, in less than one month.

Thinking they were on to something, Paul and Griffin used the profits to track down the beach vendor and order some more. They quickly sold those as well. They divided up their responsibilities: Griffin would build a website and sell online, Paul would start calling on local stores. They ran this business out of their apartment. They used the profits to sustain a meager living and continued to pour every dollar into new inventory. The more people they contacted, the more product they sold. Then they brought in unpaid student interns to help. Today, their multi-million-dollar business is thriving, and they are still running the business lean.

KEY TAKEAWAY

As an entrepreneur, you need to figure out ways to conserve your resources while you keep moving forward. As you build your start-up, examine every opportunity to leverage all possible resources so as to maximize your opportunity by spending as little cash as possible. Leverage everything.

CHAPTER FIVE

Rapid Prototyping, Right Now

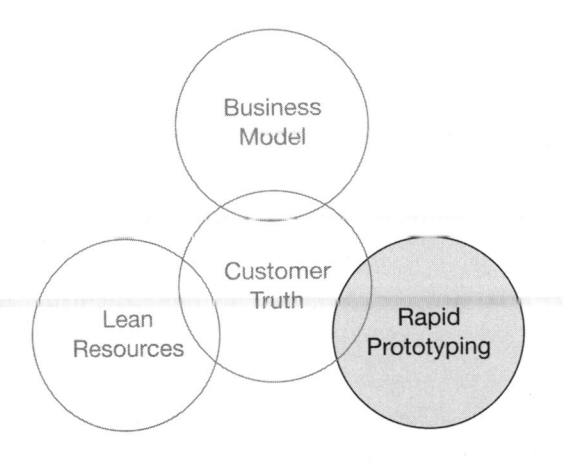

To move fast, you need a rapid prototype of your product or service. Let's review the advantages, tools, and resources available for the rapid prototyping of your product or service, as well as the testing with real customers to get that crucial initial feedback.

There is simply no better way to judge the viability of a product or service than to actually *test* it. And, with the tools and resources that are available today, there is no excuse for not rapidly testing that product or service. Indeed, entrepreneurs have all benefited tremendously from early customer feedback, whether it's good or bad. Quite a few entrepreneurs hold out and delay introducing that first version until they feel it's perfect. Guess what? It will never be perfect.

There will always be another feature you want to add or revise, or some other enhancement you feel is important. Think: *minimum viable product*. This means the acceptable, early version of the product or service that will meet the customer's needs. You can always improve the product later and add all those features "you think" the customer cannot live without.

> *"If you are not embarrassed by the first version*
> *of your product, you've launched too late."*
> **—Reid Hoffman, LinkedIn co-founder**

You *can't* always launch your company at the right time—in that perfect opening in a marketplace window. But if you delay, the window could close or, worse, a competitor may jump through the open window with a minimal product and gain the first-mover advantage. That competitor begins to get traction, receives customer feedback, and then introduces a second, improved version of the product while you are still diddling with yours. Now, that competitor is getting something even more crucial: market share and a leadership position in the product or service category.

I remember the first version of LinkedIn when I saw it in 2007. I thought, *What's the big deal? It's okay, not outstanding design but pretty functional.* But LinkedIn got the early traction and just kept making improvements on the fly, and that's why they are the market leader today. Who is even second?

RAPID PROTOTYPING TO FAILURE

You need to get over your fear of failure. I know, we have all been primed since childhood to succeed at whatever we do. But, honestly, the times we have learned the most have been when we failed. You couldn't keep your crayon colors inside the lines? Some of us got better at it or else we became artists. You lost an important basketball game in high school? You learned that life's not always about winning, it is about competing and the fun that can be.

I teach a creativity and innovation entrepreneurship course at San Diego State University, and one of my biggest challenges is getting my students to open up, to think creatively, and to take risks. They have all been taught how to get good grades and to please adults and peers. They are hesitant, though, to open up and share their ideas, mostly in fear of being ridiculed or laughed at. But the course is designed to reward individuals and teams who provide a "quantity" of ideas, not the best idea. That's when they open up and throw out all kinds of suggestions, and they begin to collaborate with no fear of being shamed. Guess what? The solutions they come up with are amazing.

FEAR OF FAILURE, SO WHAT?

Why do I bring up fear here in a chapter on rapid prototyping? Because most people fear failure and therefore they move too slowly when they should be creating a rapid prototype of their product or service. If you are going to be an entrepreneur, you can't fear failure.

> *"Life is like riding a bicycle. To keep*
> *your balance you must keep moving."*
> **—Albert Einstein, letter to his son Eduard, February 5, 1930**

You can respect fear and try to keep it in bounds; the important point is to understand the cost of entering late into the marketplace. I mentor more than 20 entrepreneurs, to one degree or another. In my classes and on-campus programs, I reach more than 2,000 students each year who could be entrepreneurs someday. I also meet quite a few potential entrepreneurs in the community. Here is what I say to all of them:

- You have only one life. Live it.

- Quit living the life you think you're supposed to have; live the life you want to have. Whatever you want in life, your work ethic will help you achieve it.

- Experts get rewarded and are invited to more opportunities.

- Fears of risk and failure are mostly in your mind, and who controls that?

- You were not born to do a particular thing; do what you want to do.

- Embrace and learn from failure; along the edge of failure lies potential greatness.

As Thom McElroy, co-founder of Volcom (see Chapter Nine), would say with respect to your career, "Design your luck."

I like to tell students and entrepreneurs that I am not special. I am just a hard-working person who put in a lot of effort to get what I wanted. I was not born to be an entrepreneur. But I became one at the early age of 37. I met three people who excited and scared me. We took the risk and together we ended up building what became a $1 billion company. You know what happened? I looked back and I felt so foolish, realizing I had spent years working for others because I thought that's what I was supposed to do.

I don't regret anything I did. But becoming an entrepreneur made me realize that a person really can do what he or she wants to do. You just need a solid skill set, a good idea, some vision, some passion, and a team. So, get over your fear and embrace the idea of rapid prototyping to learn whether you have something worthwhile. If you fail, so what? Learn from the experience and move on to the next solid idea. If you win big, though, remember to pay it forward someday.

GET YOUR RAPID PROTOTYPE GOING

As mentioned in the previous chapter, there are lean resources available to help you build your rapid prototype. The key is to consider exactly what you need to build or acquire to have your prototype product, and then evaluate the people in your network who might help you build it or acquire it. Here are some suggestions; it's not meant to be all-inclusive but, rather, a solid thought-starter list to get you moving:

People

When it comes to leveraging people, the first question I ask would-be entrepreneurs and students is, "How strong is your network?" Being able to leverage your network will help you directly or indirectly by connecting you to people who can help you. Need to find that great programmer or software architect? How about that nutrition expert? What about the designer you need to design your product? Your network, and the extensions of that network, could be the means for getting an idea moving toward prototype.

An example of this network potential is a local entrepreneur named Samantha, who had a solid idea for a mobile application but no money or programmers. I told her we had two graduate-level mobile applications classes at the university, and introduced her to the professor. After the meeting, the professor liked Samantha's idea so much that he had two students build the initial prototypes, for both Android and iPhone. What was the cost? Zero. Granted, that won't always be the case; but you need to leverage all the people resources you can so as to produce your prototype rapidly.

Internet Tools

There are a variety of either free or low-cost solutions available in what I call the Internet tools; I described these in Chapter Three. For example, want to gauge potential customer interest in a new type of product or service? Utilize a website-building tool, search-engine optimize it to bring it to the attention of potential customers, and measure their reactions to your product or service, either in traffic or actual purchases.

For example, Jon was a student with solid online marketing skills who would track trends and throw up a website (using WordPress) almost every other weekend, just to see what would happen. He once did this with a clothing product and received almost $3,000 in orders. Did I mention he did not even have the product? I'm not advocating his approach, of course. Jon scrambled quickly, found a local manufacturer, and had the product made, then shipped all the orders in less than a month. But his experience shows how volatile and productive the Internet can be; the tools are out there for your creative use. The point is to test something, move quickly, and learn if you are on to something that will sell in the marketplace.

Online Platforms

With online platforms like Amazon.com or Etsy, you can quickly create a product prototype, or even acquire a few products, and test them with real customers in these online marketplaces. For instance, another local entrepreneur, Suzan, started selling her hair-care products using Craigslist as a way to test-market them.

Have you built a mobile application? Get it uploaded in both the Android and iPhone marketplaces, spread the news on Facebook, and see what happens. Have an online tutoring service you want to give a trial run? Create a private tutorial video and post it on YouTube or Vineo, and gauge the reactions. Key here is not to think of all the reasons why you *can't* get something prototyped; think of the ways you *can* get it done.

New Technologies

It seems that every day we hear about a new technology hardware or software, or even a service that enables something to be done better, faster, and at a lower cost. For instance, today's mobile applications seem to be threatening so many of our more established technical "ecosystems" (i.e., GPS in applications/smartphones versus older

Garmin devices). So, you have to pay attention to what's changing in a marketplace to fully understand the potential.

The reason you have to pay attention is that new technologies entering a marketplace create ripples that you might not initially see. Those ripples grow and spread into new products and services. For example, how many entrenched point-of-sale system-based companies cringed when Square launched its payment hardware (wireless 1-inch square device) and software application? This one company is changing an industry, allowing people to create virtual "cash registers" with their smartphones and tablets, all wirelessly. To grasp the significance of this development and see other opportunities that may appear, you would have to study how people and business owners are using Square and anticipate what they might need next.

The same thing is happening with mobile applications, e-commerce website platforms, and other innovations that enable sales via the smartphone. The smartphone is the platform for more and more commerce, as well as the more established social media uses. So, ask yourself: What opportunities does this create? And as soon as you have a view of those opportunities, build your product or service prototype.

Manufacturing

I discussed manufacturing resources in the previous chapter. The key here is to know what resources are available locally to help you build your prototype. But expand your region to a 150-mile radius so you'll have greater options. For example, Leeann was an entrepreneur here in San Diego who came up with a design for a woman's foldable shoe. Finding no resources locally to build her prototype, and not really wanting to go offshore for the prototype, Leeann visited the Los Angeles fashion district. By walking around and meeting designers, vendors, and small business owners, she located a supplier who helped her both design the prototype and produce it.

Look into "rent by the hour" manufacturing and engineering facilities. They provide the equipment and some resources, and charge you by the hour to help you build your prototype. Some enterprising entrepreneurs rent or use idle commercial kitchens to test and prepare the food products they are prototyping. Marcus, an entrepreneur who is selling those popular new stand-up paddleboards, approached a local surfboard manufacturer in San Diego; instead of seeing Marcus as a competitor, the surfboard founders crafted an agreement whereby they will make the paddleboards for him, as well as their own surfboards. This will save Marcus quite a bit of money and time, as he had been outsourcing the manufacture of his paddleboards to an offshore operation. So, think alternatively; sometimes, your competitor in theory is not your competitor in practice, they might become your supplier.

Another way to perhaps get your prototype manufactured is to leverage your local university. In addition to the incubators, look at the resources that exist there and understand that students often need to create products in order to complete their degree requirements. This work touches on departments of engineering, computer science, nutrition, film, and graphic design, among other fields. Build a relationship with a professor, and perhaps your product can become someone's senior project.

Lastly, as I mentioned in Chapter Three, 3D printing is revolutionizing the way we produce products. It surely is revolutionizing the way entrepreneurs produce prototypes. If you have not investigated 3D printing yet, do so. It may well be the most cost-effective way for you to rapidly produce your prototype.

MARKETPLACES, LOCAL AND ELSEWHERE

True rapid prototyping is also testing your product or service in the marketplace that contains your niche customer segment. I have seen the right product proposed to the wrong people, and consequently the product fails in early tests. So make sure you are testing your product in the right place, at the right time, and with the right potential customers.

Remember, *initially* your customer is not everyone in your large customer segment; your customer is in the niche target segment that houses early adopters or influencers. If your product is successful with them, they will carry you to the rest of your customer segment.

I was working with Claudia, a young entrepreneur who was designing out-of-home digital display advertising based on GPS, and she was convinced her customer was marketing agencies who would offer her product solution to their customers. She spent the better part of a year trying to build relationships in that industry, meeting with agency personnel, but she got nowhere. She did have a very good working prototype. Based on advice from another entrepreneur, she started approaching small local business owners who were located near large outdoor displays, or who could hang digital displays in their business windows. Her sales took off. So, know who your initial target customer is, and that will drive the marketplace where you need to be.

GETTING IT OUT QUICKLY, SOME EXAMPLES

Rapid prototyping is not just about the prototype and the testing, of course. It's emblematic of a state of mind: *get something to market quickly*. And, then, based on customer feedback, you can improve your product. It could be a mobile application, an article of clothing, a new food item, an e-commerce website—it really does not matter. What does matter is that you get into the marketplace rapidly. Don't wait. Fail fast or win big.

Here are some examples of rapid prototyping involving real entrepreneurs and real products. Learn from their experiences. And, don't assume these companies are or were all successful. The purpose here is to show how they rapidly prototyped their solutions in order to rapidly test them in their marketplaces.

Eco-Friendly Designer Sunglasses

Jenny was extremely interested in social causes, and she relished the opportunity to associate real products with a great cause. That's not too dissimilar a stance from Tom's Shoes, which could serve as a business model. But Jenny wanted to have a more "personal" impact. So she did a fair amount of research to identify some serious needs in the world that could benefit from additional resources. (Remember, Jenny had no product yet, not even an idea for one.) Her focus was on *who* the company could benefit.

As part of the research, Jenny found out that more than 1 billion people in the world experience some form of blindness, either from lack of access to prescription eyeglasses or from untreated cataracts. The solution was simple: offer used prescription eyeglasses or provide $15 cataract surgery. Jenny determined that this goal would be the company's mission.

Now, she needed to identify a product that would generate the revenue to fund this cause. Jenny examined several potential products but nothing seemed to resonate. One day, while walking through an airport, she "saw" the product. Well, not actually *the* product but something very close: sunglasses. Jenny investigated producing sunglasses with sustainable materials, a matter also of great concern to her. She also felt that a socially responsible company would strike a chord with a large market.

After some more research, Jenny determined the sunglasses would have to be manufactured offshore. Not knowing who to contact, she used several supplier portals to reach out to about five manufacturers, and she provided product specifications and asked for bids. Not one of the manufacturers would meet all the product specifications, but one manufacturer came close. They sent some samples that looked, well, they looked cheap. But Jenny had never dealt with any type of a manufacturer before. So, instead of looking for help from other entrepreneurs who had experience with offshore manufacturers, she ordered 300 pairs (which was the minimum order), paying for them with $1,500 borrowed from a family member.

The glasses arrived and they actually looked good. Jenny had someone make a display rack and she convinced one local store to carry and sell them for $49.95 each. They started selling almost immediately. The glasses were made from sustainable material, a fact that was clearly displayed on the rack, as well as where the proceeds of the sale would go. This trial run convinced Jenny that there was a marketplace for this type of socially conscious product and a way to support her cause.

Web-Based Software Tools Solution

I met Andrew when he was a graduate student at San Diego State University. He was a very talented student, with two engineering degrees, and was just about to graduate from the MBA program. Big problem, though. He had absolutely no idea of what to do after graduation. He could easily get a job, but that was not what he wanted. Infatuated with the idea of creating a start-up company, and absolutely fascinated by the Internet, he set out to learn everything possible about online marketing.

In an effort to eke out a living, he worked as an online marketing consultant for small business owners. But the freelance consulting world does not always provide a consistent paycheck, and after one year Andrew was struggling. In desperation, he redesigned the consultancy website, grew frustrated with the website platform tool functionality, and taught himself two programming languages so as to craft a better set of solutions for the website. Then, Andrew search-engine optimized the new website.

Within 24 hours, Andrew received about five emails from online developers, who inquired where they could buy the two "widgets" they saw on the website that had simplified some programming tasks. He reached out to me, asking, "What should I do?"

I said, "Can you figure a way to package and sell that programming code?" He said he could figure it out. That night, Andrew redesigned his website yet again, now as a software tools company. He set up a PayPal account, figured out a way to secure and deliver the programming code, and without anyone else to help, started taking payments and shipping "programming tools" via email to other developers.

The feedback was positive and word leaked out into the wider developer community. Soon, Andrew was receiving 50 emails or orders a day and he had to redesign the website yet again to handle the increased demand in a more sophisticated environment. This convinced Andrew that he was on to something and he set about building a software tools company aimed at serving web developers.

Solar-Powered Products

Adam has never worked for anyone. He came out of school about five years ago as a graduate student and, even while in school, he leveraged trends and sold commodity products in online marketplaces. His business model was built on providing products that were in demand, could be produced at a slightly better quality than available to the online mass market, and could be offered at a reduction of at least 30 percent in cost. All this while offering a gross margin of at least 60 percent. Most of the products came from offshore manufacturers and were fulfilled by the online e-commerce companies. It was a very virtual business model. There were no real employees, just a series of college interns.

   In the United States, solar products initially were available for either large commercial or residential installations. But about two years ago, Adam noticed that some portable consumer solar products were entering the online marketplace. They were simple, not yet high-quality solar smartphone chargers and the like. Not knowing exactly which product made sense to package as his own to sell online, Adam headed to the largest technology trade show in Asia. At this trade show, Adam was overwhelmed by all the new technology products, but he sought out the best solar products he could investigate that were intended for the consumer marketplace.

   At one booth, Adam noticed an eight-panel solar array, a multi-plug black box, and a nice 16-inch metal attaché case. While talking to the manufacturer, Adam, via his smartphone, looked for a mobile solar product like this one online and found only one other, offered at a major consumer brand website—and it was at a significantly higher price. Adam asked the manufacturer about product costs, minimum orders, and availability.

Within 60 days, Adam was selling this mobile solar charging kit on two online e-commerce marketplaces. He was receiving one order per day at $299 each from each marketplace. That's $4,200 per week in orders. After just two months online, with reviews and search-engine optimization, the number of orders Adam was receiving had doubled.

Healthy Natural Food

Every now and then, accident meets opportunity and a product is born. The key is knowing it when you see it. Sally saw it, but as a young child. Only later did she act on it. As a young child, Sally's father loved the idea of eating natural foods, including fruits and vegetables. One day, quite by accident, her father discovered a simple way to dehydrate a certain fruit. Armed with his experience, he constructed a natural dehydrator and began to dehydrate this fruit for his family, including his children.

Fast-forward 15 years, and one of his children is now a world-class triathlete. Training and competing all over the world, Sally always carried with her some dehydrated food to consume while competing. Other athletes noticed what she was eating, and asked if she could bring them some, too. She started bringing a larger supply of the dehydrated food to the competitions. Shortly before "retiring" from competition, Sally looked into how she could produce this dehydrated food on a larger scale, thinking she might be able to turn this simple product into a business.

Sally visited several plantations back in her home country to understand the product harvest, dehydration process, and packaging and distribution. Using a lean resources mentality and a rapid prototype philosophy, Sally harnessed a small amount of friends and family money and created some sample packages. She then began to sell them at athletic competitions. The feedback was positive, but Sally sensed that this might not be the true market. She was selling her product and getting good feedback, but not really making any money.

The triathlete market has strong and reputable influencers, but is small in number, and this product needed high-volume sales to become a sustainable business. It also needed to be sold to health-conscious consumers with a fair degree of disposable income. So, Sally found a freelance designer to redesign the packaging to be consumer friendly and appealing to a wider group. She started visiting local independent health food and organic food stores, pitching her product to store managers. Sales were slow initially, but she gained more independent stores and also began selling the product online. Based on word of mouth and attractive packaging, Sally landed placement in a regional health food chain. Now, her dehydrated fruit is in over 1,000 stores.

ENTREPRENEUR INSIGHT

In an MBA class several years ago, a team of students decided they would create a business plan around a passion they all shared. They all loved the ocean; a couple of them were divers. They also loved music. They discussed how they would like to listen to music while they were in the water. One of the students had an engineering undergraduate degree. The business plan itself got a B-. Not deterred, almost on a lark, the group set out to build a waterproof casing that would house an MP3 player and be able to withstand the pressure typical of their dives.

The guys took it on a dive trip—and it worked. Then, a potential investor looked at the prototype and commented that it was ugly (essentially a black box). The team conducted more research and decided to broaden their market to include anyone who was getting wet. They went to an offshore manufacturer and had a beautiful waterproof smartphone case designed, then showed this prototype to retail store managers. With no sales history, the retail store managers were hesitant to order the product. So, the team built a website and started selling their case online; they also sent some cases to celebrity surfers, swimmers, and runners for comment. Their sales took off.

KEY TAKEAWAY

You don't really know if you have a company until you have created a product or service prototype and have sold it in the marketplace. That is, you can't improve a product unless you get customer feedback. And you need to move faster than potential competitors. So, create a prototype sooner rather than later.

CHAPTER SIX

The Whole Customer Truth

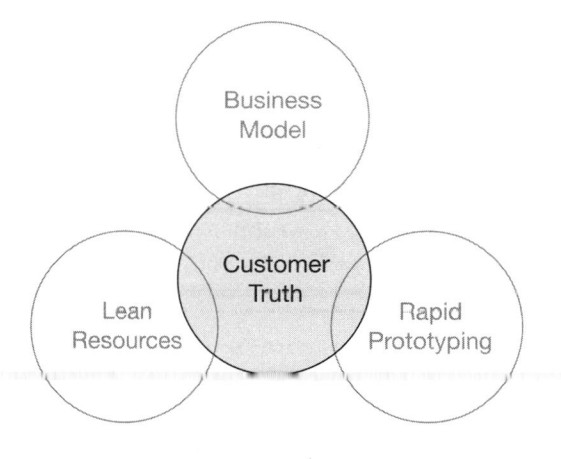

I have met tens of thousands of customers, and you know, I never get tired of meeting them. And neither should you. Today, my customers are college students who are taking my entrepreneurship courses and participating in the Lavin Entrepreneurship Center programs. I get constant feedback through interactions in the classroom and through student surveys. The feedback has both quantitative scores and qualitative comments. I read everything. I look for little aha's—those comments that point toward ways to improve my courses. Just when I think I have created the world's best entrepreneurship course, a student comment will let me know that I have yards to go.

The LeanModel Framework works just like this. Customer truth is the heart of the model. There is a logical reason for this. As an entrepreneur, your biggest ally is your customer.

> *"Right or wrong, the customer is always right."*
> **—Marshall Field, entrepreneur and founder**
> **of the famous Chicago department store**

If you connect with your customers and keep your product or service promise, those customers will help you with your marketing. They will write solid reviews. Via word of mouth, they will tell others about your product or service. But ignore them and you do so at your peril. A great idea that's poorly executed with customers is in real trouble. Especially if those customers have the option to buy the same type of product or service from your competitors.

Recently I conducted a workshop on customer loyalty and service for a local company that owns 10 retail service stores catering to small business owners. Sam and Irwin, the two founders of that company, felt their business was at a critical juncture. Started with just five employees six years ago, the company now had over 100 employees—and yet, they felt something was lacking. They sensed complacency had crept into their business and so they were concerned.

Sam and Irwin assumed the problem lay with training. At the workshop, I talked to the employees about what was actually happening in their marketplace—how it was getting competitive and going to get even more competitive in the next five years. That their customers had choices, and that the only differentiator for them was how the employees served their customers.

> *"I've learned that people will forget what you said, people will forget what you did, but people will never forget how you made them feel."*
> **—Maya Angelou, American poet**

I asked the employees to name a company they admired for its customer service but that they had never met an employee. They were puzzled for a few minutes. Then one person said, "Amazon.com." I asked why. The person said, "They keep their promise." The rest of the employees in the room murmured their agreement.

I then asked them, "How many of you make and exceed a customer promise every day? How many of you ask your customers what will make them happy? How many of you ask them what you can do to meet the customers' needs?" The room fell silent. They got it.

Sam and Irwin have instituted myriad "customer best practices" in recent months, including better training, greater hiring standards, and motivational reward programs for their employees. They now conduct face-to-face and quantitative surveys with customers every week. With no additional marketing dollars spent, their business revenue went up by 20 percent in a very competitive market. They are now aggressively seeking "customer truth."

WHY YOU NEED TO DELIGHT YOUR CUSTOMERS

In your lifetime, you will probably never meet an Amazon.com employee. So why is this "brand" so successful? Because "they" never stop responding to their customers' needs. In 1996, when Jeff Bezos asked our agency to handle all of Amazon.com's marketing, we spent months trying to figure out how to differentiate this "brand" from its competitors. We didn't even work on any creative elements for the first three months. Instead, we focused on the customers: on their expectations and what would delight them.

We were stalled in some initial brainstorming, so we asked ourselves, "Who delights *us*?" After some discussion, we all agreed it was boutique hotel concierges. So we went and visited them. We saw how they remembered and greeted people who came back repeatedly to stay with them. How they provided reviews for local restaurants. How they retrieved newspapers for guests. How they asked people if they enjoyed their stay. This "concierge mentality" was designed into the Amazon.com experience. It's based on seeking customer truth so that you discover how to delight your customers.

EMBRACE CUSTOMER TRUTH

To fail fast or win big, you need to understand your customers. You also need to embrace the idea that customer feedback, or as I like to call it, "customer truth," is critical to the success of your company. Marketplace graveyards are littered with companies who quit listening to their customers (e.g., Blockbuster, Blackberry, Borders, A&P food stores, Nokia, Kodak, Tower Records, Circuit City). Many other large companies are teetering on the edge of failure and will almost certainly be gone in the next few years. On that short list are, perhaps, the cable companies, entertainment and fast-food companies, and several retail brands that are simply not paying attention to their customers or the developments in their marketplaces.

It concerns me that most students and a number of potential entrepreneurs don't grasp the importance of knowing *everything* about potential customers. Okay, you can't know everything—but how about knowing some things that are important? When I get pitched an idea, my first questions are about the potential customers. Invariably, the entrepreneur or student begins to falter. Perhaps it's because of my extensive branding experience and long marketing career, and my entrepreneurial and turn-around careers, but I believe it's critical to know as much as possible about current or prospective customers.

In this chapter, I share my insights and experiences with branding and marketing as it relates to customer truth. Then, I give some examples of my (and, quite frankly, any entrepreneur's) expectations and work ethic in regard to customers and their buying preferences.

MY EYE WAS ON THE CUSTOMER

Early in my career, I landed on a marketing agency account team that was working with Cadillac, the luxury car division of General Motors. Honestly, at age 27, I did not know or have anything in common with 45- to 70-year-old Cadillac customers. I reviewed all the research on hand, looked at all the customer survey data, and still felt I did not know enough about Cadillac's products, dealers, or customers—and felt I knew even less about the competition. So, in that first year on the account, I spent a good deal of my spare time visiting Cadillac and the competition's dealerships. I examined showroom environments, met with salespeople, and sat with customers in the customer service lounges. I asked customers about their product and service experiences, and inquired about how many Cadillacs they had owned and why.

Later that year, with my customer insights, I started to make strategic recommendations to the Cadillac management. When they asked where I had gotten the basis for my recommendations, I indicated that I had met with more than 250 customers that year. The Cadillac senior marketing manager I spoke to said he doubted the entire management team had met with that many actual customers. That was an amazing revelation to me. Was it any wonder that Cadillac suffered in the '80s and '90s?

Another agency assignment had me working with Nikon. I loved their cameras. But I knew very little about who was actually buying those cameras and the accessories. So I spent my free time in camera stores. I went to photography trade shows and events. I met with professional photographers. I took a photography class for beginners. I bought a Nikon camera from a local dealer. I learned a lot about the entire "ecosystem" that Nikon lived in—more importantly, I learned about their customers and the trends in the marketplace. These insights led me to recommend an accessories sales and marketing strategy that yielded millions of dollars in additional annual revenue for Nikon, and even more satisfied customers.

Later, when I worked with Apple to support their education-channel sales with marketing strategies and campaigns, I met with education-channel salespeople at computer dealers. Then I visited elementary and high schools to better see who was buying Apple computers and why. How were schoolchildren using Apple computers in their classrooms? I learned much about what was happening in education and how Apple's vision for educating children included using powerful hardware and software technology. All this insight allowed me to recommend marketing strategies to drive Apple's education market share higher. And Apple's early focus on its customers in the education marketplace made them a dominant player in education. It's also a classic branding and marketing strategy: get to future customers early and often, so as to continue selling to these customers your future products, like music players, smartphones, and tablets.

When I was a partner at CKS | Partners, I developed the integrated branding and marketing strategy for Amazon.com. Initially, I was insanely curious about who was actually buying books online in 1996. Our team spent months studying several marketplaces, including the traditional bookstores and the emerging online e-commerce platforms. We worked very hard to understand who was actually buying books online initially; but better yet, we wanted to know who we needed to target that would lead us into a much larger marketplace. All of our research led us to a core influencer target market smaller than 2 million people (i.e., those who love to read books, are early technology adopters, have higher incomes, etc.). Our research showed that, in the United States, they were located mostly in just two or three states and perhaps four key cities. This close focus on adopter customers, plus our attention to building a customer "experience," allowed us to increase Amazon.com sales explosively over the next two years.

YOU ARE NOT THE CUSTOMER

You can't assume you know what a customer wants or needs just because you are launching a start-up to serve that customer. Why do so many entrepreneurs assume they know what a customer wants or needs—even when those entrepreneurs themselves do not fit the target segment profile? And even if you *do* fit the target segment profile, don't assume you are the customer or know more than they do. You don't. You want to know why? *You are not the customer.*

Ever meet a 45-year-old entrepreneur who is running a start-up making products for 18- to 25-year-old customers? Or, the reverse? And, if you did, did you ever wonder what he or she was thinking? Here is some advice for entrepreneurs: never assume you know your potential customer. Ever. That realization will force you to do several things:

- Always be researching the marketplace and trends.

- Base your decisions about customers on as many facts as possible.

- Surround yourself with other people who might have customer insights.

- Relentlessly visit the customer environment.

Many entrepreneurs and company founders speak as though they are customer experts—yet yesterday, before the launch of their start-up, they were engineers, nutritionists, lawyers, accountants, programmers, and the like. When did they transform themselves into the customer?

Here is what you should do to learn more about your potential customers. Ask these types of questions:

- What are the customers' ages, incomes, and sexes?

- Where do they live?

- What do they live in?

- What kind of music do they listen to?

- What kind of car do they drive? Lease or own?

- Where do they shop for clothes?

- What kind of food do they buy?

- How do they use technology in their lives?

I could go on, but you get the point. You need to understand your customers. You can't assume that you know everything—or even any-thing—about them. You can't *pretend* that you are in the mindset of your customer.

REAL CUSTOMERS, REAL SITUATIONS

Here are real situations from real entrepreneurs and how each of them handled learning more about their potential customers.

Fashions for Young Women

Two young entrepreneurs, Paul and Griffin, now 26 years old, started their company about four years ago with a fashion product aimed at and purchased predominantly by women, ages 15 to 22. In order to understand and maintain their knowledge about this marketplace, they immerse themselves in their customers' world. They attend trade shows and events that feature fashion buyers so they can hear from professional buyers about what is trending, what is selling, and what is on the horizon in terms of fashion. They attend fashion shows and even music concerts, always noticing what women that age are doing and wearing.

Probably one of the most important things that Paul and Griffin do is have about 10 interns working in their business who are in their customer's demographic. These interns update the website, talk to distributors, and deal with store owners. They are responsible for the fashion blog on the website and they also update the company's social media. They provide Paul and Griffin with feedback and insights about the product design based on trends they are noticing. It's a great way to stay in touch with customers.

Internet Photo App

Duncan is a 35-year-old serial *mobile* entrepreneur. He had previously created and sold two companies that produced mobile services and/or applications. His third company came about when Duncan began to notice the staggering number of photos that were being uploaded to the Internet. By some forecasts, this numbers more than 1 billion each day. As Duncan's team started to investigate this marketplace, they noticed a "sweet spot" of customers ages 14 to 18 who were very active in uploading their photos. The more time they spent looking at this demographic, the more convinced they were that they had a couple of potential products for this marketplace.

The other people in this start-up were about the same age as Duncan and were software programmers, so they set about building a prototype. Within about 45 days, they had a functioning prototype that worked on a tablet, and they began to test it with friends and family who were in that target age range.

No one liked it. They felt the features of the application were not that great. Seven out of 10 potential customers said they would not download it, even for free. So it was back to the drawing board. This time, the team brought some college freshmen on board in the design and functionality process, and they started to get some real insights. They rapidly built another prototype and tested it with 16- to 19-year-olds. This test customer group liked it and made some suggestions that a younger demographic would like. Based on that feedback, they built the final product for the smartphone platform and launched it. They are on track to receive 2 million downloads this year.

SEEK CUSTOMER TRUTH—RELENTLESSLY

Think *relentless*, which means "unending." Though you're just forming your start-up, embrace the idea that you'll continually be in the customer's environment to learn about that customer. You're not just there at their purchase decision, but also wherever the actual customer environment is, whether that's a retail location, a dealership service area, a restaurant, a local mall, an airport, or a grocery store. You will be studying customer behavior so well that you will "know" what they might do next.

Additionally, you will need to visit your competition and see how they treat their current customers, and what could possibly be improved. For example, in my own company, which dealt with creating new brands or launching new products, I regularly walked into the customer environment and met with real customers. I never relied exclusively on the survey research data or third-party industry reports. I needed to "feel and touch" the customers. I needed to see what they felt, to better understand their patterns, to really get insights into trends that were affecting them or those that were potentially starting.

As an entrepreneur, you need to be zealous in your approach to understanding your current or potential customers. Just as an aside, it would have helped Blockbuster Video and Borders Books if they had watched or listened to their customers!

ANTICIPATING WHAT CUSTOMERS WANT

"Customers may not always know what they want, but they are never wrong." I believe the biggest piece of advice in that adage is simply to accept that customers are never wrong. They are not always right, but they are never wrong. As an entrepreneur, it may seem easy to believe you know what customers want. If you had been Larry Page in the days before Google, perhaps you would have agreed with him if he had said, "Online search results suck and I am going to make search results way more relevant." I don't think you would have needed to conduct customer surveys to find out that people wanted a better, more relevant search engine.

> *"It's really hard to design products by focus groups. A lot of times, people don't know what they want until you show it to them."*
> —**Steve Jobs, co-founder, Apple, Pixar, Next**

Other times, though, it's more difficult. Say, you are designing a car that will take three to five years to get to market. Do you ask customers what they want, not knowing what is going to be going on in the world five years hence? Are customers designers? Do they even know what they want versus what they need? If you read the Steve Jobs quote, it seems to make sense. And yet, do you want to hedge your bets and get some direct customer insight? Of course, but it can't drive the decision-making process. It can add insights or help confirm some assumptions, however.

In my 20 years' experience, I cannot recall a time when focus groups or customer surveys were used to design or determine final products. To be honest, I am not a big believer in focus groups. Can 12 people really determine the fate of a product or service? Seems risky to me. I have used focus groups to look for an "aha" moment or to discover something we missed, but not as an affirmation of what we were going to do.

When we landed the Amazon.com account in our Portland office, we never utilized a focus group to test our designs or recommendations. We looked first at crafting the "soul" of the website brand around the idea of a helpful concierge. Once that was done, we looked at the early adopters who were buying books from Amazon.com and we did research on the next possible customer segment—that is, who were the next most likely 2 million buyers? We discovered that they were people who loved technology and who read voraciously, both books and daily newspapers like the *Wall Street Journal* and the *New York Times*. They were also people who traveled. They lived primarily on the coasts, and had higher household income. They were thought leaders and influencers.

When Jeff Bezos gave us the majority of his funds that he raised in the first venture capital round for marketing, he asked about the marketing strategy. We told him about our concentric rings expanding outward from a core target customer base of early adopters. We explained that we were going to use heavy print advertising carefully and word of mouth to drive Amazon.com revenue upward. He asked if we were advertising online. We said no. Initial advertising would be in just three regional publications, on an almost daily basis in smaller strip ads. That and public relations would drive the "fever" we intended to build.

We also suggested implementing an affiliate program whereby targeted companies would place online book banners on their websites for free in return for a simple commission on referred sales. We did not have enough money to do more advertising or marketing. Bezos was nervous; honestly, so were we. But we were also excited and sure we were on to something big. Time to fail fast or win big. We launched the campaign and sales exploded.

Here is the takeaway. *You need to know your customer.* You need to know your customer's environment. As much as possible, you need to know what your customer aspires to be or do. You need to have an ability to have conversations with that customer. But I agree with Steve Jobs. If you asked customers to design an MP3 player, it wouldn't look like an iPod. Most people might not ask for a 1,000-calorie burrito from Chipotle. Or a $75,000 electric car like a Tesla. Customers will tell you what they want, but not what they need.

The truth about customers is that they will tell you what they *don't* want. Customer truth is a funny thing. They are not always right, but customers are never wrong. Gather as much information as possible. Listen well and, it is hoped, you will give them what they need. If not, they will tell you the truth.

CUSTOMER SEGMENTS AND POSITIONING LADDERS

If you are looking to create a start-up company, or perhaps you see an opportunity to enter a disrupted marketplace, focus on *exactly* that target market segment, and conquest that segment first. You can't take on the whole marketplace. As I mentioned in the beginning of this chapter, when entrepreneurs tell me they have a product that will revolutionize civilization, I ask them the size of the marketplace. They say 100 million people. When I ask them to identify the target segment, they say 100 million people.

Seriously, cut the marketplace into several segments, target the early influencers/innovators, then the early adopters, then the next segment, and then the next larger segment. If you get into the third segment, you are probably going to have a successful company. The sparks of customer segment networks will be firing and word of mouth will be driving sales. (If you want more insightful information on customer segments and networks, read *The Tipping Point* by Malcolm Gladwell.)

One of the best books I ever read on how people categorize "brands and products" in their minds is *Positioning: The Battle for Your Mind* by Al Ries and Jack Trout. Amazing book, simply written, powerfully explained. Their premise is that we, as humans, organize everything into neat little categories in our brain; they call those categories "ladders." Based on their research and insights, Ries and Trout determined that most consumers usually remember the *top three* brands or products on every ladder, and that if your company cannot or will not penetrate the top three, you better reconsider your positioning strategy or that marketplace.

In other words, if you can't be in the top three brands or products in the customer's mind, consider creating another ladder. Think of the top five car-rental companies; in less than five seconds, say them out loud. Did you get past three? Here's another example. When a new company wanted to enter the rapidly growing bottled-water market, they knew there was no room in the customer's mind for another water brand on the "water" ladder. So they created a new category ladder—vitamin water—and placed themselves at the top. The company? Vitamin Water.

So, before you create your product or service, examine the market and your potential placement in the customer's mind. Is there room for another brand/product or do you need to create a new ladder?

YOUR BRAND MATTERS—BIG TIME

I have worked with some amazing brands. Kellogg's, Mercedes Benz, American Express, Nikon, Apple, Mazda, Powerade, Amazon.com, Nike, Widmer Brewing, Yahoo!, Mercury Marine, John Deere. When you are in the midst of working on an existing brand, or even launching a new brand, you don't notice all the great elements that make up that brand. Until you meet the customers. They remind you of why a brand is great—or not.

When I ask entrepreneurs about their brand, they say, "What? Do you mean our logo?" If that is the answer, I know they don't understand the power or importance of branding. Rather than spend hours explaining it, I suggest they read *The Brand Gap* by Marty Neumeier. I explain that the brand exists inside of customers' heads, that it is what they *feel* about the product or service. I explain that people need to trust that brand and that trust comes from reliable and consistent "delight" with the product or service. Entrepreneurs must very carefully "craft" their companies or product brands with the utmost design and care.

> *A great brand is one that
> customers believe has no substitute.*

As an example, the Apple iPhone is really just a smartphone. Tear off the outer shell and what do you see? Integrated components. So why do most iPhone owners *love* their iPhone? Why do they *feel* so good about this product? More important, why do they feel there is no substitute for their phone?

Put as much care and attention into every element of your company, both product and brand, as Apple has. Or, as I often say, it costs just as much to design a weak brand/product as it does to design a great one.

CUSTOMER SATISFACTION AND LOYALTY

When I ask entrepreneurs what they will do to ensure customer satisfaction and loyalty, they often explain what they will do *after* the sale. But that is too late.

Take the time to grasp the impact of a poorly designed and launched product or service, and how word of mouth will negatively impact future sales. Market researchers have noted that people who are disappointed in a product tell *five times* as many people about their disappointment than they do when they are satisfied.

That negative talk can have a significant effect. With today's online reviews, that number can grow exponentially. On the positive side, though, consider the *lifetime* value of a satisfied customer.

For example, Starbucks has done exactly that. Assume that you have bought one Starbucks latte per day, five days a week and 52 weeks a year, for about 20 years. At a price of $4 per cup, that's $20,800. That's serious money, and it's all tied to customer loyalty.

Here are four major guidelines for building exceptional customer satisfaction and establishing ongoing loyalty with your future customers.

- *Meet expectations:* Sounds simple, but quite a few entrepreneurs get this wrong. It's your customers' expectations you are trying to meet, not your own expectations.

- *Exceed expectations:* Unless you are launching a monopoly, you'd better plan on exceeding your customer expectations. This is what builds brands and keeps competitors at bay. Just meeting their expectations does not.

- *Delight the customer:* Here is where the brand really gets built. When you delight the customer, you build trust. That trust gives your customer the feeling that your product or service cannot be substituted.

- *Great customer service:* This sounds really simple but so many companies get it wrong. They get hung up on hierarchy, policies, processes, and everything else that prevents great customer service. Recall every bad customer service experience you have ever had, and then don't do that.

When you create and launch your start-up, everyone around you will be watching. They will be taking their cues from you. You are creating the company culture. Will you be respectful to customers, or do you just want their money? Strive for the highest levels of customer satisfaction, and loyalty will follow.

LEARN TO LISTEN

You will never satisfy 100 percent of your customers 100 percent of the time. You should try, of course, but it won't happen—statistically. So, knowing that, figure out all the ways you can have conversations with your customers and really listen to them.

> *"If a customer's calling and they have a gripe, don't you think they kind of enjoy the fact that I picked up the phone and talked to them?"*
> **—Jim Sinegal, co-founder, Costco**

It's not always what you do wrong that matters so much as how you fix it. Walk among your customers. Before Jim Sinegal, former CEO and founder of Costco, retired, he routinely visited more than 150 stores per year. That's almost 200 travel days annually. He would also stop in at competitors' stores. He had no problem talking to employees and mingling with customers. When he was asked why he did this, he would often say, "Seeing is believing."

If you called Costco to complain about something, there were certain times where he would answer the phone. I know. I called him once, expecting to get his assistant. He answered the phone instead. That's my kind of entrepreneur.

CUSTOMER TRUTH IS DEFINED BY THE CUSTOMER

If you use Google to search "customer truth," you will get a smattering of results. Some entries will talk about how "communities" of consumers are now providing brands with "community truth"—that is, a sentiment the entire community believes to be true. Other entries touch on the economic impact of "customer loyalty" and the financial value of a customer. Several cite the "moments of truth." This might be industry jargon, but it's the process a customer goes through with respect to purchasing a product or service. This process happens in stages, and you should be aware of them.

- *Zero Moment of Truth (ZMOT):* Created by Google, it's what people search for and find after encountering the initial message that directs what they do next. Google spokespeople would say this is "that moment when you grab your laptop, mobile phone, or some other wired device and start learning about a product or service you're thinking about trying or buying."

- *First Moment of Truth (FMOT):* Introduced by Procter & Gamble (P&G), a great retail products and marketing company, it's what people think when they first see your product, and the impressions they form when they read about it or see images of it. This is the critical point when shoppers can become customers.

- *Second Moment of Truth (SMOT):* Furthering P&G's philosophy, it's when people feel, think, see, hear, touch, smell, and (sometimes) taste, as they experience your product or service. This is not the first time but occurs after several purchases.

- *Bernie's Moment of Truth (BMOT):* This is my spin on the moments of truth. It's how the brand listens or reacts to a customer problem. It could be as simple as an order of coffee or as large as a washing machine. If that "brand" steps up and satisfies you, you will be with it for a long time. If it disappoints, you are gone.

How many of us have purchased a product or service for years—and then it happens. The product quality suffers. Poor service, with an attitude. Or just a lack of respect. I know people who will not even *consider* a certain luxury car brand owing to a fallout with a salesperson or a service adviser over a relatively small problem. And that's even after owning that brand for 15 years! They will also tell everyone within earshot why that company is a failure.

As an entrepreneur, you will need to understand the consequences of *not listening* or *failing to deliver* excellent products and services to your customers. Define "customer truth" any way you want; but understand its power. If you are listening to your customers, you will improve your product and service, based on their collective feedback. If you ignore their feedback, you won't have to worry about improving your products or services—because you won't have any sales.

Also, refrain from defending your company with statements like, "The customer just does not know how to read instructions or use the product properly." Remember, "Customers are not always right, but they are never wrong." Believe that and you might win big.

ENTREPRENEUR INSIGHT

In 2009, Kevin and Mike set out to create a mobile application that they felt would be on the cutting edge for mobile consumers. It would have several features, one of which was the ability to use location as its core attribute. They spent more than one year building the application, and when they thought it was perfect, they invited a core set of friends and family to try the application on their smartphones.

The user feedback was not good. In fact, those family and friends said that the application felt cluttered and overrun with features. But there was one key feature that they liked. And Kevin and Mike listened to this "customer truth." They agreed that they needed to pivot the company. So they started over and built a new application around the one feature everyone liked: photos. Instagram was born.

KEY TAKEAWAY

You do not have to be a brand or marketing expert to understand the impact of customer satisfaction and loyalty. You do not have to have 10 years of customer service experience. You do need to listen to your customers and accept their truth about your product or service.

CHAPTER SEVEN

Entrepreneurs Have a New Investor: The Crowd

The traditional ways of creating and launching an entrepreneurial company still exist, but the world of start-up funding has changed forever. Crowdfunding, which is the raising of capital primarily through an Internet platform in the form of donations or investments in exchange for future products, lending, or equity, has opened up opportunities never before possible. But let's take a look at what was available and now what is possible.

TRADITIONAL SOURCES OF FUNDING

In the not too distant past, if you needed some money to start a business, you'd look to several sources. First, you might examine your savings or, perhaps a bit riskier, you could leverage your credit card. Or, you could turn to friends and family to raise the necessary funds.

Another traditional source of funds, if you had collateral, was local banks. Possible funding, based on your product, could come from angel investors, those early investors in a company. With some initial growth and revenue, it might be possible to attract private equity investors. Finally, based on the opportunity, industry, and size of the marketplace, you might receive funding from venture capitalists in exchange for an equity stake in your company.

However, funding was difficult to get outside of friends and family. Angel investors typically only do one to three deals per year and average in the $25,000 to $100,000 range. Through their formal and informal networks, angel investors might be exposed to 15 to 20 companies per month. That wasn't great odds for an entrepreneur. With venture capitalists, the odds for an entrepreneur receiving funding went down further still. Industry averages show that venture capitalists invest in about one out of every 400 deals they review. While their funding levels are higher, $3 to $7 million per investment, they are extremely selective. Especially after the Internet bubble of 2000 and the recession of 2008, venture capitalist firms have been hesitant to look at start-ups that are not yet generating significant customer adoption or revenue.

> *"The way to get started is to quit talking and begin doing."*
> **—Walt Disney**

THE NEW SOURCE FOR FUNDING

The entrepreneurial ecosystem of financial support has radically been altered. In 2009, a new form of funding arrived, called crowdfunding. Crowdfunding is when hundreds or thousands of independent people "crowd together" to fund a project that usually entails the launch of a new product by a start-up company. Initially, crowdfunding was project based, providing entrepreneurs with capital, usually in the form of "advance sales" of a product. Early crowdfunding platforms included IndieGogo and Kickstarter.

But now, based on legislation related to the JOBS Act of 2012, crowdfunding has been extended to include new equity platforms that can be used to raise capital in exchange for equity stakes in these companies. The Securities and Exchange Commission (SEC) will finalize the rules for equity crowdfunding sometime in late 2014.

To better understand crowdfunding and its potential impact, let me walk you through how we got here and exactly what it looks like, how it works, and how to maximize use of crowdfunding platforms. Then, we will look into the future and see what impact this new type of financing will have on the entrepreneurial ecosystem.

Why Crowdfunding?

The crowdfunding platforms arrived on the scene for several reasons, including technology, efficiency, opportunity, and available investors. Did we ever imagine just how powerful the Internet would be and how it would impact almost everything we do? I am not sure we even fully understand the power of this platform today, which has so changed the world and will continue to do so forever.

It is relatively easy for an entrepreneur to launch a crowdfunding campaign and raise thousands, if not millions, of dollars in a relatively short time. This is due to the simplicity and power of the technology built into the infrastructure of crowdfunding platforms and their easy use by millions of potential supporters and investors. Using a web-based crowdfunding platform, you can quickly build a campaign, and using social media and email tools, you can communicate that campaign to an immediate network of supporters and beyond.

As mentioned in regard to other aspects of selling, the Internet and its related technology have helped marketplaces become more efficient. And crowdfunding is no exception. Just as we saw the rise of companies like Open Table, Etsy, Airbnb, and Über, we now have the crowdfunding platforms like Kickstarter and OurCrowd. For some entrepreneurs, crowdfunding will provide the necessary funding for their start-ups.

Several industry analysts forecasted that crowdfunding would reach over $5 billion (project and equity crowdfunding) by 2013. Kickstarter alone has raised over $1 billion for entrepreneurs since its founding in 2009. While that's pretty impressive, several experts predict that the size of the crowdfunding marketplace over the next few years could quickly rise to over $300 billion, based on forthcoming government regulations. That's a pretty significant marketplace for investment opportunities and it increases the odds for entrepreneurs.

The Power of Crowdfunding

So, what's actually driving all these crowdfunding platforms? *The democratization of buyers and sellers.* Every marketplace needs sellers (in this case, entrepreneurs) and buyers (for entrepreneurs, investors) to be successful. In the past, unless you were an angel investor or venture capitalist in a certain city or region, you simply did not "see" these investment opportunities, or could not invest in the best of the start-ups. For example, how many angel investors or venture capitalists get to privately review those start-up investment opportunities?

As of 2010, there were 462 venture capital firms registered to do business in the United States. With an average of four or five key partners, that's only about 2,000 people. Similarly, several sources cite there are about 400,000 angel investors in the United States who were active and made investments in small companies during the years 2003 to 2008. Now, compare those figures to just one crowdfunding platform, Kickstarter. They indicate that, since 2009, 5.7 million people from 224 countries have donated money to fund at least one project.

In short, the new investors are here, everywhere. They are you and me, and everyone else who has access to the Internet and some dollars to invest. For entrepreneurs, this presents an amazing new funding opportunity.

AN OVERVIEW OF CROWDFUNDING

Crowdfunding is having a dramatic impact on entrepreneurship. In particular, equity-based crowdfunding will likely fund a large number of start-ups that will result in a new pipeline of crowdfunded ventures. The newer equity-based model of crowdfunding, finalized with SEC rules, will likely permit both accredited (those with $1 million in assets or at least $200,000 annual salary) and nonaccredited investors to acquire shares in privately held businesses in exchange for a portion of those entrepreneurs' ownership stake.

In the broadest sense, crowdfunding is the use of the Internet to raise capital by way of small investments from a large number of investors. Though it remains difficult to accurately predict the long-term implications of crowdfunding, it will be a permanent fixture on the entrepreneurial landscape. Optimists, such as serial entrepreneur, angel investor, and venture capitalist Alan Hall, of *Forbes* magazine, see a bright future:

> What, then, have these business owners been doing for funding? They've been relying on credit cards and home equity loans, funding vehicles that have been severely affected by the struggling economy. So if they can't get money in those ways, and the banks aren't going to help them, we need to recognize that crowdfunding, as it grows, will play an increasingly critical role in the entrepreneurial ecosystem, with or without the participation, wisdom and safeguards of more-established investment vehicles.

This is consistent with what many believe will be a fundamental shift in the options available to entrepreneurs for raising capital.

Let's review the three major types of crowdfunding platforms that exist today: reward, debt, and equity.

Reward

Reward campaigns exemplify "traditional" crowdfunding on platforms like Kickstarter or IndieGogo. In exchange for some reward (a discount, freebie, product pre-order, or other item), individuals contribute money to an organization, project, or company. These platforms are here to stay.

Kickstarter is an online crowdfunding/equity platform where the majority of the funds raised go to the entrepreneurs. If a campaign is successful, Kickstarter takes a 5 percent fee and the funds are dispersed through Amazon payments, which entails another 2 to 3 percent fee. Kickstarter was launched on April 28, 2009. It's a for-profit company based in New York City, and as of late 2013, it had just 69 employees. But astoundingly, its platform has helped entrepreneurs obtain more than $1 billion since its inception. And the amounts seem to grow larger each year.

When I first heard of this crowdfunding platform in 2010, I did not think entrepreneurs could raise serious amounts of money this way. That changed on May 18, 2012, when the Pebble Watch start-up raised a staggering $10,266,845 even though its goal was just $100,000. An entrepreneur might be able to raise $10,000 to $20,000 from friends and family, but $10 million is way beyond most friends and family. Experts believe the funds raised for the Pebble Watch, a Bluetooth-enabled wristwatch that communicates with a smartphone, were from people just placing their orders in advance for a potentially cool watch.

But are these new "voyeur investors" just flexing their rewards muscles before they venture into the "selective ring" of equity crowdfunding? Here are a few of the reward crowdfunding platforms that every entrepreneur should review:

- IndieGogo: Initially launched with a focus on film, will now do almost anything.

- RocketHub: Launched with more arts projects in mind; also focused on sciences.

- Peerbackers: Launched for innovators and entrepreneurs, now includes young adults.

- Kickstarter: The most well-known and popular, but has a reputed tough review process.

Debt or Lending

When it comes to investment crowdfunding, most people immediately think "equity." But there's a whole other side to investment crowdfunding, known as *peer-to-peer lending* or, more commonly, debt-based crowdfunding. Through this model, entrepreneurs may utilize *debt crowdfunding platforms* for a loan in return for interest that is due based on the funding agreement.

Similar to bank loans, these arrangements call for applicants to demonstrate creditworthiness, or an ability to responsibly handle and repay debt. In many cases, this poses an obstacle for start-ups, which have yet to fully establish credit. However, if you are generating sales and cash flow, this might provide the right opportunity to finance a future inventory order. With that said, creditworthiness is not the only factor lenders consider, so those rejected by large institutions still have a shot at obtaining funding this way. For entrepreneurs who do acquire loans through debt-based crowdfunding, the interest rates vary so shop around for the best rates and terms.

The debt-based crowdfunding process differs from platform to platform. Generally, you need to submit an application for review. Often, debt crowdfunding platforms outline very specific criteria, so double-check that you are qualified before submitting any information. Some platforms measure the financial risk of a given opportunity as a part of their own project valuation, similar to how other investors might perform due diligence. For this reason, not every application is accepted.

To get started, check out some of these debt crowdfunding platforms:

- Funding Circle

- Lending Club

- Prosper

- Zidisha

- Index Ventures

Overseas, there are many thriving platforms to investigate as well, such as Assetz Capital and Zopa.

Equity

Equity crowdfunding is an amazing alternative compared to traditional sources of funding. It is the collective effort of individuals (investors) who network and pool their money, usually via Internet crowdfunding platforms, to support entrepreneurs by providing investment capital in the form of equity.

Equity crowdfunding can also refer to the funding of a company by selling small amounts of equity to many investors. At the moment, equity crowdfunding is the least developed form of crowdfunding, but that is changing rapidly. Once the proposed SEC rules are finalized, this area of crowdfunding could explode.

The new equity crowdfunding rules proposed by the Securities Exchange Commission were a long time in coming. Equity crowdfunding first saw the light of day as a provision of the JOBS Act, which was passed and signed into law in April 2012. While these rules will be finalized in 2014, here are some of the early suggested rules proposed by the SEC in October 2013:

- Start-ups cannot raise more than $1 million in any 12-month period.

- Investors with annual incomes or a net worth below $100,000 can only invest $2,000 or 5 percent of their annual income or net worth, whichever is higher.

- Investors with annual incomes or a net worth above $100,000 can only invest up to 10 percent of that annual income or net worth.

- Transactions must be conducted through an intermediary. Intermediaries include registered brokers or a new type of entity called a "funding portal."

This new fundraising method will most likely be used by early-stage companies looking for initial capital to fund the start-up, and not all crowdfunding platforms will offer this type of fundraising to entrepreneurs.

The move toward equity crowdfunding is exciting for start-ups and entrepreneurs, who now have an alternative to traditional venture capital. Some of the equity crowdfunding platforms that you should review are:

- OurCrowd
- Grow Venture Community
- Micro Ventures
- Angel List
- CircleUp

There are quite a few more. Do your due diligence; utilize your network and select the platform that you feel will help you succeed.

CROWDFUNDING CAMPAIGN TIPS

After reviewing successful crowdfunding campaigns on both rewards and equity-based platforms, I can provide some insights and tips that may help you better prepare for your crowdfunding opportunity.

For Reward Campaigns

Crowdfunding platforms specializing in projects or rewards like IndieGogo or KickStarter could be an amazing fundraising strategy for entrepreneurs. Review the platform and their rules carefully. And if you do proceed, study other successful projects. Expert advice includes creating a video and using social media vigorously. Here are some key tips to get you started:

1. *Give people a great story.* If you are going to raise funds to produce a product or service that you are passionate about, then tell them a great story. Put some passion into it and a bit of personality. Don't go over the top, but give them an "emotional" reason to support you.

2. *Set your funding goal carefully.* Get the funding you need to launch and test the new product or service. Some small start-ups set reasonable goals of $10,000 to $40,000 and achieve their objective. Others go for $75,000 and only raise $47,000 and so they receive nothing (you have to hit or pass your goal to receive the funds).

3. *Create a great video.* Videos seem to be one of the top reasons people decide to fund a project. Don't be an amateur and use your iPhone or webcam. Find someone qualified, a film student or a freelancer, and create a compelling video with some creativity and personality.

4. *Design a set of rewards that make sense.* Some entrepreneurs think that by having 37 reward levels they will cover just about every possible funding scenario. No. Simplify to just 10 rewards or fewer that are easy to understand and, more important, that you can fund.

5. *Prepare your production plans ahead of time.* If you are using a manufacturer to help build your product, plan ahead of time to use your campaign funds once you have them. Get multiple bids and understand the production and shipping time lines.

6. *Spread the word online.* Entrepreneurs need to create word-of-mouth awareness that goes beyond your friends and family network and that you can reach via online marketing tools. Research ahead of time and identify blogs, websites, LinkedIn groups, and the like where you can spread the word.

7. *View your email campaign as critical.* Take the time to craft a strong set of emails (at least five to seven ahead of time) that will simply but powerfully tell your story. Provide links to your crowdfunding project and your video. Provide updates

on how the project is doing. Use a simple but emotional close. Give supporters a reason to care.

8. *Welcome your new job.* Entrepreneurs frequently underestimate how much time they need to spend on their 30- to 45-day campaign. It's a full-time job that needs to be cared for almost every day. Put in the time and reap the rewards.

9. *Backers are supporters, supporters are backers.* Once you have people funding your project, keep them engaged. Constant updates, maybe some behind-the-scenes photos or videos of the product development—anything to make them feel special so that they spread the word to other potential backers in their own networks.

Reward or project-based crowdfunding platforms are amazing things. Where else can you raise money or pre-sell your product, perhaps raise $50,000 or more, and not give up any equity or incur any debt? Entrepreneurs, take advantage of this crowdfunding platform if you can.

For Equity Campaigns

Equity-based crowdfunding is bringing entrepreneurs a brand-new group of investors and is changing the way early-stage capital is invested in given industries. This new way of funding will enable entrepreneurs and investors to connect quickly. While there are many benefits, such as going to market faster, having more investors to pitch, and greater potential strategic relationships, let's examine how to build a solid equity crowdfunding campaign.

1. *Pinpoint your lead investor:* Most of the investing crowd will follow a lead investor, so focus on cultivating and closing a lead investor whom others will respect or trust. If you're fortunate, some of your early investors are either well known or their credentials will establish some social proof when recruit-

ing additional investors. Move on to lesser-known investors only after you have your lead investor locked up.

2. *Protect your equity:* Don't give up too much equity if you don't have to. Just because you're new to the process, that doesn't mean you have to comply with unfair requests. For example, some investors may ask for board seats. Unless the investor is hugely strategic or invests more than 50 percent of your target amount, think long and hard about such requests. Ask the investor if he or she would like to help you in an advisory role.

3. *Step wisely in the crowdfunding jungle:* Equity crowdfunding, however it develops, will be closely regulated and monitored. If you're raising money by offering equity through one of these platforms, you're required (or the platform is) by law to verify that the investor is accredited (rules still being finalized). Some entrepreneurs are using third-party companies that offer a certification service to identify accredited investors. This could be a significant time-saver and can keep you in compliance with the SEC.

4. *Spend your time well:* Manage your leads based on this simple formula: after a couple of emails and conversations, estimate the chances your prospective investor will invest. Prioritize your time and focus on investors with the best potential. Avoid investors who are overly concerned with near-term profitability rather than in building a brand and capturing market share quickly. Long-term strategic investors who have industry or marketplace connections are the best possible investors.

5. *Communicate frequently and well:* Investors don't like to be kept in the dark or be surprised. Send investors frequent updates about investments, major endorsements, any positive public relations, and potential news on product concepts or prototypes. Most crowdfunding platforms have automated tools

you can use. Also send personal emails for good measure to smaller groups and to specific investors with more details than public "status updates."

6. *Solicit feedback often:* In addition to your investment, potential investors might be reviewing quite a few deals. Many have launched successful businesses and some have even had successful company sales or exits. Sometimes it's best to ask for advice before you ask for their money; a good investor will let you know if he or she is interested. By soliciting valuable feedback, you're sure to avoid wasting each other's time. Even if you don't get a check, at least you've increased your odds with the next investor by improving your pitch and presentation.

7. *Build trust and confidence:* Hone your people-facing and speaking skills. If you need to take a public speaking seminar, do it. You must build rapport with investors. Investors have to believe in you, and that's directly reflected in how much you believe in yourself and in your company's potential. Good investors can smell uncertainty and hesitance, so don't think that you can fool them. Be honest, sincere, and passionate.

THE BENEFITS OF CROWDFUNDING
TO AN ENTREPRENEUR

As an entrepreneur, you are looking to create a start-up company. There are a number of important benefits that crowdfunding offers you.

Greater Access to Capital

At an early stage, you may think that outside of your own network, you can raise capital only from accredited investors, venture capitalists, and banks. Crowdfunding is a great alternative way to fund a venture, and it can be done without giving up equity or accumulating debt. The crowdfunding platforms allow you to raise funds from the investor community in exchange for simply providing tangible products or equity.

A Way to Hedge Your Risk

Starting up a company can be a very risky and challenging journey. Besides finding sufficient funding, there are always expenses that are impossible to forecast, challenges in market validation, and other people who want a piece of your venture to help get it off the ground. Utilizing crowdfunding hedges these risks and serves as a valuable learning experience. Crowdfunding as it is today allows you to gain market validation and avoid giving up too much equity before going all out and taking a product concept to market.

It's Also a Marketing Platform

An active crowdfunding campaign is a great way to introduce your start-up company's overall mission and vision to the market, as it is a free and easy way to reach numerous customers. Quite a few crowdfunding platforms incorporate social media tools, making it painless to get the word out to prospective customers or investors. This provides the potential to receive thousands of "organic" visits to your website from customers and potential funders. These users are also important for viral marketing, as they have the ability to share and spread the word to their network connections.

It Provides Proof of Concept

Showing potential customers and investors, and convincing yourself that your venture has received sufficient market validation at an early stage, is hard. However, crowdfunding makes this possible. The first question that any subsequent angel or institutional investor will ask will often be along the lines of proof of concept, and a good way to gain some respect and credibility is to show them that your venture had a successful crowdfunding campaign. This instills trust and integrity toward a venture in its early days and potentially validates the opportunity.

It Offers Crowd Brainstorming Opportunities

One of the biggest challenges you as an entrepreneur face is to be able to cover all the holes that a start-up might have at an early stage. By having a crowdfunding campaign, you engage the crowd and receive their comments, feedback, and ideas. This feedback is extremely valuable, as it can help you uncover some aspects of your business proposal that were previously unthought of. It could also inspire new ideas for the product or service and improve the opportunity for success.

It Builds a Loyal Customer Base

A crowdfunding campaign not only allows you to present a business and a product, it also gives you the ability to share the message and the purpose behind it. People who view your campaign and decide to contribute or invest are people who believe in the success of your company in the long run. In essence, these people are early adopters. These early adopters are important to every business, as they can spread the word and assist in the future success of your company.

It's Free Public Relations

The momentum created by successful crowdfunding campaigns attracts other advisers and potential investments from traditional investors, as well as attention from the media. Success stories make for interesting reading, and writers are always looking for them. Crowdfunding is unique and interesting in these early days, and countless entrepreneurs who have been successful with it have seen larger success and exposure as a result.

It Brings in Pre-Consumer Sales

Launching a crowdfunding rewards campaign gives you the ability to pre-sell a product or concept that you haven't yet taken to market. This is a good way to gauge customer and marketplace reaction and analyze the market to decide whether to pursue or pivot on the opportunity. Also, in a rewards campaign, the excess funds generated (your revenue versus the cost of the product) are yours to keep and use as you see fit to grow your start-up.

It's Free

On all-or-nothing crowdfunding platforms (meaning that you get the funds raised only if you reach 100 percent or more of your funding goal) there are so many benefits and usually no fee to participate. If you set a goal and don't reach it, there is usually no penalty. If you reach your goal, most platforms charge between 5 and 8 percent in total fees. For an equity crowdfunding platform, they likely take a fee of 10 to 15 percent on the capital raised from investors. This may change as equity crowdfunding platforms become more competitive in the future.

THE FUTURE OF CROWDFUNDING

I was asked in a recent interview if I felt that, in regard to crowdfunding, investors would be fleeced by aggressive entrepreneurs. My reply was simply: "Investors who don't do their homework always risk losing their investment. But what qualifies just a handful of angel investors, or even venture capitalists that are located in certain regions of the country, to be the only ones looking at early deals? Why can't these deals be pitched online and investors from all over the United States, or world, make a micro investment in the next Google or Pebble Watch regardless of location?"

In the next few years, you will see hundreds of investment firms rushing to offer crowdfunding equity platforms. Perhaps even some super angel investors, venture capitalists, and private equity funds will establish their own platform so they can make micro investments in early-stage companies. In time, things will settle down and crowdfunding will flourish as a major alternative source of funding. If the expert predictions are even close to correct, calling this a $300 dollar marketplace, then you as an entrepreneur might be better able to raise more money and give up less equity in this new open marketplace.

ENTREPRENEUR INSIGHT

Since 2009, three young would-be entrepreneurs named Coby, Mike, and Braydon have been exploring and tinkering with elements of 3D printing, including the rendering software. An engineering student, an entrepreneurship student, and a young firefighter, respectively, they all pursued a passion for tinkering. And 3D printing caught their eye and imagination. But they could not understand why everything was so expensive. Almost cost-prohibitive. So they looked to learn from others and share what they had learned.

At one point, based on their research, it became evident that no one in the emerging industry was interested in building a low-cost 3D printer that most people could afford. So that became their goal. Enter Kickstarter. They created a Kickstarter campaign and set a goal of $49,000, and hoped for the best. They got the word out and received quite a bit of public relations. Their campaign closed on February 1, 2013, having raised $649,663. Since then, they have prototyped their printer and are testing it with potential customers.

KEY TAKEAWAY

You have several options to secure funding for your start-up. Examine your options carefully and then choose the best one for you. Investigate the new crowdfunding platforms as at least one of those options might be viable for you. That way you get the funds you need and keep as much equity as possible.

CHAPTER EIGHT

Opportunity Is Here and Everywhere

In addition to teaching entrepreneurship courses at San Diego State University, I am a director in the Lavin Entrepreneurship Center on campus and I participate actively in the local start-up community. So I am approached often by students and entrepreneurs (or would-be entrepreneurs) seeking my advice. More often than not, I am not interested in their idea per se. Instead, I ask about the marketplace, the industry, key trends, and their initial target segment. Most of the time, they don't have all the answers and I send them off to acquire more information about their prospective opportunity. In this chapter, we look at opportunity from different perspectives and determine what an entrepreneur can do to prepare for such an opportunity. In particular, we'll cover the following:

- The Entrepreneur's Epiphany

- Targeting a Market

- Why Marketplaces Matter

- Types of Opportunities

- Key Elements in Finding Opportunities

> *"The entrepreneur always searches for change,*
> *responds to it, and exploits it as an opportunity."*
> **—Peter Drucker, management guru**

CAN YOU "CREATE" AN EPIPHANY?

In his book *Myths of Innovation*, Scott Berkum says that most people do not understand how entrepreneurs create new companies. He describes the myth of the "epiphany," that light bulb that goes on in the head of an entrepreneur in the middle of the night. He reminds us of the expertise rule: that we begin to become experts in a given field only after we spend at least 10,000 hours (an average of 7–10 years) working on that craft or industry; at that point we begin to see things clearly and, especially, more opportunistically.

The epiphany is that sudden realization of a relationship, that merger of dissimilar thoughts. But as Berkum points out, it usually comes only after many years of familiarity with a subject. So, how can an entrepreneur increase the chances of having an epiphany that could potentially yield a new idea? Here are a few ways:

- *Become an expert in your area of expertise.* Berkum highlights several inventors or entrepreneurs who worked for years to solve a problem or to create a product. The 10,000 hours to become an expert sounds like a big number, but it's only 7–10 years, assuming a normal work year. That time is probably less for would-be entrepreneurs, since they don't have normal work years. But regardless of the time involved, use your expertise to leverage that knowledge and experience to create a new type of product or service.

- *Look for emerging or disrupting trends.* When Jeff Bezos observed the emergence of the Internet, he saw the potential for a new distribution platform for selling products. He just needed to validate that enough customers would exist in this new marketplace. He initially sold books to build a loyal set of customers so that he could then sell them everything else as well.

- *Surround yourself with different people.* If you want to generate ideas, don't hang around with people who are exactly like you. If you have a business background, seek out film makers, artists, programmers, and designers. Look for common passions and share ideas with them. Different perspectives on the same subjects can create a robust environment for discovering what's next.

TARGET A MARKETPLACE

So, you are a would-be entrepreneur but you don't have an amazing idea for a start-up. Here is a thought. Rather than straining to come up with an idea, examine a large and/or growing marketplace thoroughly; get to know its workings so well that you might well surface a problem or opportunity. Only then should you try to create that new product or service. Sound backwards? I don't think so.

The best example of this happened recently, when Nick, a former student of mine, walked into the Entrepreneurship Center to talk to me about creating a company. Here are the highlights of our conversation, from his point of view:

"So, I want to create a company and I remember what you said about focusing on a growing or changing industry, a large customer segment, and some key trends that were driving change either in the industry or with customers. So, I recently bought a dog. I like dogs. Out of curiosity, I did some research on the pet industry, and here are some facts I discovered. There are more than 70 million dogs in the United States. The size of the pet industry in the United States is over $50 billion; and it has had about 4 to 6 percent annual compound growth over the past 20 years, and is forecasted to continue growing at that rate into the foreseeable future.

"It seems that the baby boomers, 78 million of them, are replacing their college-age children with pets when the kids go off to college. According to the latest research and people I have been talking to, the baby boomers are treating these pets as family members. So, correspondingly, they are spending more dollars on better pet food and health-care costs for their pets. I have visited more than 10 pet stores in the past two months, and the one thing I have noticed is that no major brands dominate the stores. It appears that the pet stores carry a lot of products and product categories seem fragmented, with no dominant market-share leader. So, based on everything I have learned, and I am not sure about the specific product or service yet, but I am going to create a company that will exist in the pet industry."

I wanted to reach across the table and hug him. He is following his curiosity and instinct and getting to know the marketplace. He is studying the customer and understanding key trends. He is becoming familiar with the possible changes coming in the pet industry. Whether those changes are new types of organic dog food, using technology to track lost pets, or providing health-care services that improve the health of pets, he is doing the due diligence required to explore an opportunity.

Quite often, it's this pursuit of information about a market that is lacking in potential of newly minted entrepreneurs. The serial entrepreneurs, though, seem to have figured it out.

IDEAS COUNT, MARKETPLACES MATTER

People pitch me ideas all the time. In my role as Director of Programs at the Lavin Entrepreneurship Center, I listen to students pitch me their ideas. So, I get to hear lots of interesting ideas. As I discussed in Chapter Three, for a new idea to work, you need to have identified the niche segment of your target market that would care about your product or service.

I am a big fan of large, emerging, or disrupted marketplaces. The notion that entrepreneurs just need to come up with new ideas to create a successful company may work sometimes but I have learned that it's the marketplace that matters most. You can have an amazing idea, but if there is no clear market opportunity, it might just as well be worthless. The worst thing you can come up with is a great idea that only 1,000 people can buy or utilize (works if you are SpaceX). So, a better way to look at entrepreneurship is to start with the marketplace, then follow with the idea, usually a solution to a problem customers are having.

It sounds backwards, but follow my logic. Imagine Larry Page (co-founder of Google) doing his thesis on the relative value of accurate online search results. He studies how many people search each day (millions), and he realizes that this number is only going to get bigger. Now he has a big marketplace in mind (people who use search engines) and he wants to solve the problem of getting better organic search results. Remember: Big marketplace, Big idea.

More than 70 million dogs in the United States.
78 million baby boomers. More than $50 billion in
annual industry revenue . . . see any opportunity?

For instance, consider Nick's story mentioned earlier. He described the size of the pet industry in the United States. That it was consistently growing at between 4 and 6 percent annually, and that there were more than 70 million dogs in American households. That's a big marketplace for pet products. If you were to note the emerging trends, like upscale urban kennels, better-quality pet food, GPS technology for locating lost pets, and so on, you could probably identify several opportunities worth pursuing. They would all need to be market-tested and examined as viable business models, but it's a better methodology for creating a start-up than thinking you are going to have an epiphany in the middle of the night.

If you have an idea, look at the potential market. How many people could buy your product or service? Is that market growing? Or, has it been disrupted by some new development? What are the key trends driving buying preferences? If you have no ideas today, that's okay. Pick a market or industry you are passionate about, and do your homework. Identify the industry and get to know the market so well that you can "see" the existing problems and the opportunities. Then craft an idea or two out of that analysis and test it with potential customers via a prototype. Based on the results, you evolve, pivot, or abandon the idea. Welcome to the world of entrepreneurship.

MARKETS, MARKETS, MARKETS

If you have ideas for new products and services, consider them in the context of their market. Markets, or marketplaces, can be a group of companies that make up an industry, a physical place like a mall, or a large group of customers. So when you think of a potentially great product or service, or perhaps a solution to a current problem, put that idea into a marketplace. Here are some simple questions to ask yourself:

- Can I easily test my idea in the marketplace?

- Is the market easily defined?

- Can I reach people in the marketplace easily?

- Is the market growing?

- Is the marketplace being disrupted?

- Is the marketplace fragmented?

With the LeanModel Framework in mind, target a favorable market or come up with a low-risk strategy in a potentially unfavorable market. You really can't put together a business strategy on an idea unless you understand the marketplace and its potential customers. The more you examine that potential marketplace, the more you will learn. You will then spot something that you can test with a Lean-Model Framework, and you'll either fail fast or potentially win big.

ITERATION, EVOLUTION, OR REVOLUTION?

Too many entrepreneurs think that, to have a successful start-up, they need to create something the world has never seen before. So, they spend a large amount of time thinking of solutions *in search of* problems or marketplaces. It would be better if they focused on large markets (customers), trends, or the disruption of a marketplace caused by an early leader or a technology shift. Then they could direct their energies toward solving both existing and future problems in that marketplace.

Let me put it into perspective. As I've mentioned before, Google was not the first search engine. Apple did not launch the world's first MP3 player, smartphone, or tablet. Facebook was not the first social media company. Chipotle was not the first restaurant to serve Mexican food. Kashi did not invent cereal. Starbucks did not create the first café. But they all have something in common. They all *iterated* or *evolved* a product or service beyond its current state. They added improvements that the marketplace both wanted and needed.

It takes something pretty amazing and insightful (or years of research and effort) to create a *revolutionary* product or service. Revolutionary products do create or change entire marketplaces and new ecosystems evolve. Examples of such revolutionary products include the refrigerator, the typewriter, the cellphone, the personal computer, the Internet, and so on. Probably only a few thousand products in the history of mankind have been truly revolutionary. Yet we have millions of products. So why do so many entrepreneurs think they have to create something revolutionary? Is there a "myth of creativity" that says entrepreneurs have to create something the world has never seen before in order to be successful? Entrepreneurs: Consider iterating an existing product or service in a large marketplace. More often than not, that is what drives most successful start-ups.

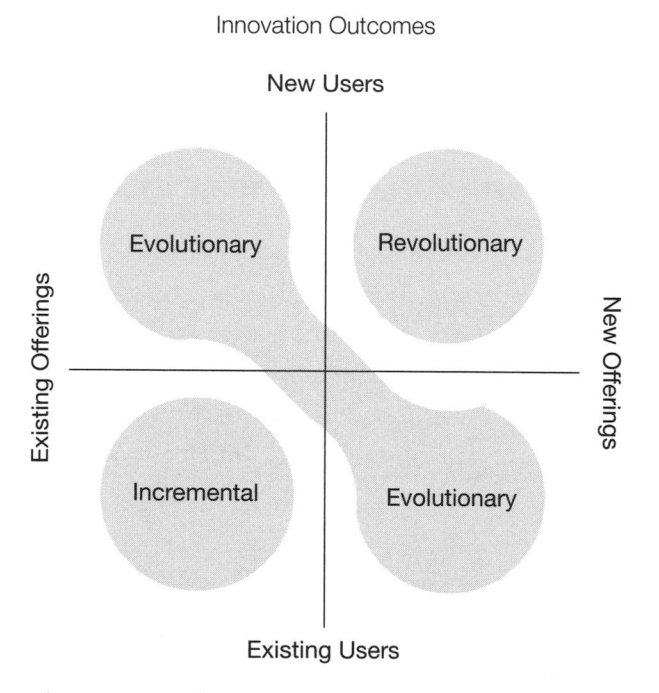

Organic growth can emerge from every quadrant of Ways to Grow. Use this tool to (a) identify the type of growth you intend to create, (b) recognize the scope of that challenge and deploy an appropriate innovation process, and (c) assess your portfolio of innovation efforts.

Figure 8.1 Innovation Outcome Paths for Recognizing Growth Opportunities

Take a look at Figure 8.1. It shows the best path for start-ups as examining opportunities with existing products and existing customers, and looking for "problems" that customers are currently tolerating in that marketplace. It forces you to understand the marketplace and its customers and the existing problems; only then do you begin to examine potential improvements or enhancements.

For example, you look at Myspace and the social media trend to make improvements to a potential Facebook; that's evolutionary. You examine the many complex and bulky MP3 players for sale in a growing digital music marketplace and you make an iPod. If you're successful, then you can grow that marketplace and attract even more customers.

Revolution in the marketplace is a bit harder to accomplish. You are wandering into a region of either creating a new product or creating "new" customers for a product or service that did not exist before. Is this where we would put Amazon.com? Prior to its appearance, books were sold in brick-and-mortar establishments or through book clubs. So, selling books was not new; selling them online was new. Ordering them via the Internet and having them delivered to your door was what was new. While the Internet was *revolutionary*, Amazon.com was an *evolutionary* start-up that leveraged the Internet and a new e-commerce and distribution system to deliver an existing product.

If you are a potential or current entrepreneur, your next opportunity is probably not going to come from an epiphany. It will come from examining large, emerging, or disrupted marketplaces. It will come from understanding the trends and defining the problems that customers are having with the existing situation. These are the kinds of questions you should be asking yourself, especially in regard to today's trends:

- Will people continue to shop using their smartphones?

- Is the $50 billion pet industry in the United States going to continue to grow?

- Will renting things hourly (i.e., cars, services, homes) continue to grow?

- Is eating organic health food going to continue as a preference?

- What other products can leverage GPS technology?

- What else will the 14- to 18-year-olds consume via social media?

- What is the impact of more than 1 billion photos being up-loaded to the Internet every day?

- What services will baby boomers need in the next 10 years?

- Do young people understand and grasp the importance of financial investing?

- What is the effect of multimedia technology on e-books?

- What is the future of online education?

- What needs to be improved regarding online dating services?

- What fitness trends will evolve and which ones are emerging now?

You can see what I am suggesting. Whatever you are passionate about, focus on the existing markets and customers, and look to solve their problems by iterating a current product or service. Then test that product or service via a rapid prototype using real customers. That investigation may yield a solid start-up opportunity. Perhaps, just by walking "down the corridor" of a product or service iteration, you may create something evolutionary—or perhaps even revolutionary.

KEY ELEMENTS IN FINDING OPPORTUNITIES

To provide some guidance in your quest for defining opportunities, here are some perspectives, tools, and resources. These should help you find, define, and perhaps position your opportunity as a new start-up in the marketplace.

Trends—Do You See Them?

Invariably, conversations about entrepreneurship turn to the subject of trends. How is it possible to identify and track so many trends in multiple industries and across so many customer segments? Well, you do need to be insanely curious. It helps if you live long enough; age and experience lend perspective to anyone's point of view. Seriously, though, my passion for and curiosity about trends (versus fads, which come and go in short periods) comes out of my branding and marketing experience.

For most of my career, clients rewarded me and my marketing agencies for leading them through their current marketplace toward where the market was going. In quite a few cases, we spotted early trends and helped create new marketplaces. In other cases, we repositioned the product or service to meet changing customer wants or needs. I learned over time to create multiple streams of information from different sources to better help me "see" trends forming. And when the information coalesced, I followed the trend for one or two years to see how it could change the industry. It is still beyond me that Blockbuster could not see the trend of watching movies online— did they never spend time with younger customers?

Look at what you and your friends, and the people around you, are reading, using, consuming, and wearing. Your sources could be the following:

- Daily/National Newspapers

- Industry Publications

- Your Professional and Personal Networks

- Retail/Online Environments

- Industry Reports on Key Vertical Industries

- Books on Emerging Trends

- Talking to People (always)

- Trade Shows and Key Events

- Online Resources Like *TrendHunter*

- Google Alerts and Google Trends

Bringing the Trend Information to You

I hear what you are saying: "I can't possibly do everything you just mentioned." Yes, you can. The question is whether you are curious or passionate enough to change an industry—or even just a neighborhood. Nothing happens by accident. You design your luck. Guess what? Being an entrepreneur usually involves hard work and perseverance.

Okay, let's assume we are all very busy. How can we leverage technology to bring information to us, or at least condense it? One of the things I recommend is routinely visiting websites that either cover trends or provide insights into major customer segments or industries. I visit their website and subscribe to their email newsletter *TrendHunter*. It tracks trends and offers perspectives on trends, as well as showcases new products. In addition, you can obtain trend reports on quite a few trends; in fact, they track *hundreds* of trends. Other online usage industry reports/websites, like ComScore, also give insights into what people are doing online or on their mobile phones. The sources are out there. Find them.

I don't know exactly how I became aware of it, but about five years ago I discovered Google Alerts. This amazing service sends a summary email of a subject term you have established via their simple registration tool. I get Google Alerts weekly on more than 20 subjects that I am tracking. They include general subjects like entrepreneurship, online marketing, and branding, as well as broad subjects at an industry level (i.e., pet industry, mobile applications) and niche subjects (e.g., GPS pet tracking). The beauty of it is that this service is free.

Because you can choose the type of information that comes to you (I just choose articles), you can quickly read what you are interested in and then discard the email. Then the next week, there's a fresh batch of Google Alerts in your interest areas that appeared online in just the last week. By the way, this selection of news is a trend in the making; in a few years, we will probably no longer search the Internet and troll websites for content, it will be brought to us. Websites as we know them now will become less valuable and "custom" content distribution will be the norm. Probably all new interfaces that will involve audio and video. I am sure there are several entrepreneurs working on this type of solution right now.

Another online tool I find useful and fascinating is Google Trends. Being the dominant search engine, Google has its privileges and they know what people are searching for all the time. Google Trends allows you to type in a search term and see how many times that search term has been entered by others into the Google search engine. The search data is by year, since 2004, as well as by country and by region. Oh, and you can compare two search terms to see the relative comparison in online searches. While online search terms are not 100 percent indicative or reliable as regards market trends, it does give some insight into what people are looking for. And if you monitor those searches, you might get an indication of a trend forming.

As an example, let's look at a Google Trends search comparison between Netflix and Blockbuster. The time period is 2004 to late 2013. If you had been tracking these two companies (based on consumer search terms" Blockbuster" versus "Netflix") between 2004 and 2006, while also looking at the trend of people watching movies on their computers, you would have observed the classic "hockey stick" trend line forming and taking off in 2007. In that year, Netflix search terms crossed the Blockbuster "line" for the first time in terms of search volume.

What does this mean? Well, everyone thinks Netflix just appeared yesterday. But the significant trends can take time to grow. And while Netflix started with very early technology adopters, little did they know that their real customer base would be 16- to 30-year-old individuals and mass-market folks who were getting fed up with their cable fees. The major competitor to Netflix used to be Blockbuster. But with Blockbuster gone, the industry has changed. Now Netflix has to innovate to keep up. By the way, I hope the cable industry has a back-up plan. Matter of fact, that probably includes the entire traditional entertainment industry as we know it today.

Understanding the Entire Marketplace

Even though we coach entrepreneurs and teach students to look for niche customer segments in an industry when they are looking to launch a start-up, I love to study large marketplaces. My definition of a marketplace is pretty loosely defined; it extends to a large group of similar customers or a group of companies that form a large industry. Invariably, both customers and industries go through change. So, usually when one new product or service invades an industry or customers adopt a new product or service, there are multiple effects. You have to step back, look at the bigger picture, and see what might happen inside the entire marketplace.

> *When you first saw a smartphone, did you*
> *"see" mobile applications and accessories too?*

Let's assume it's the year 2000 and the first smartphones have appeared in the market, touted by early adopters as the next best thing ever. We would have been looking at either a Blackberry or a Nokia, for the most part. And while we were fascinated, the price point was high and the relative speed of data over the telephone networks was still relatively slow. But history tells us two things. Prices always come down. And according to Moore's law, technology speeds double every two years.

So if we fast-forward to 2005, we start to see smartphones coming into the broader marketplace. Are they getting wider adoption? Who is buying them now? But what about the whole marketplace? At this point, did you see the mobile applications and accessories that followed in their wake—or how large those markets would become? Mobile applications did over $12 billion in business in 2012, while the smartphone accessories market was estimated at over $20 billion that year. I wish I had created Angry Birds. Or designed a smartphone case by 2008, in time to see the market really take off with the launch of the Apple iPhone.

If we had looked at smartphone searches via Google Trends in 2007, we would have seen the beginning of the upward curve that indicates tremendous consumer interest. It's not authoritative by itself, but when that is combined with all the other data and research, and discussions with customers and industry professionals, we would have seen it coming. Then we could have decided what kind of company we could create to leverage this new "ecosystem" called the smartphone.

Know the Major Customer Groups

Do you look at large customer segments? Do you even know who they are? Millennials will number more than 80 million by 2025 in the United States; that's three out of every four employees in the workplace. And I mentioned earlier that there are about 78 million baby boomers, and they feel they are not going to die. They will, of course, but in the meantime, this large customer segment is changing and helping to create several new industries. Whether its fitness, health food, financial services, automotive luxuries, technology, or home automation/monitoring, they are having a huge impact on several marketplaces right now. And they will continue to do so for the next 10 to 15 years. What do you know about them? If you spent some time studying either the baby boomers or the millennials, you will begin to see trends forming across this customer segment and into several industries. Then you can begin to analyze what new products or services these groups are going to want to consume. Do yourself a favor and gather enough information so as to determine the major trends here. Then ask yourself what opportunities exist for a start-up company to leverage one or two of those key trends. You just might win big.

Industries Changing and Emerging

For an entrepreneur, there is always opportunity. You just need to look at something hard enough. But as you look for opportunity, you need to look for gaps in the marketplace. One of the tools I have found useful is a simple marketplace quadrant chart. It uses two key attributes (important to the customer, not you). You plot the current market competitors, perhaps even your own company if you are in the marketplace. Then you look for major gaps where one of two things might be happening: (1) the marketplace is shifting due to industry players; or (2) customer wants are changing and no one is noticing just yet.

Creating a chart like this seems really simple, and it is, but it serves well as a visual reference for where companies in an industry are positioned. Unless you create a chart like this that everyone on your entrepreneurial team can agree on, you'll just have a lot of opinions from everyone.

As an example of how it works, let's look at the restaurant industry and examine the segment called "fast casual." As customers become more health conscious and want higher quality, this segment has grown rapidly and is now highly competitive. Imagine if you were a start-up and were looking at this marketplace. You would not want to position yourself in the market right next to or in the same place as your key competition. You need to look for an area of the market that has a gap, a place you can call your own in the customer's mind.

Imagine that you are a start-up called Chipotle. You know what the competition looks like: Rubios. Baja Fresh. Taco Bell. You notice that customers want something healthier, slightly higher quality, and they want it fast. So, you target an area in the market with a slightly higher price point and slightly higher quality. Then you develop a solid business model with a competitive edge via a smaller retail footprint, smaller menu, fewer ingredients, less labor to prepare, and a culture that rewards managers. I don't know if you can even recall how long Chipotle has been around, but the chain just passed $3 billion in annual revenue. For a company that was started via one location in 1993, that's pretty good. Figure 8.2 shows the chart we've been discussing.

When you see a new product enter the marketplace, look beyond the initial product and ask yourself what accessories, add-ons, applications, and complementary products or services might be driven by this core product. As I suggested earlier, if you had noticed smart-

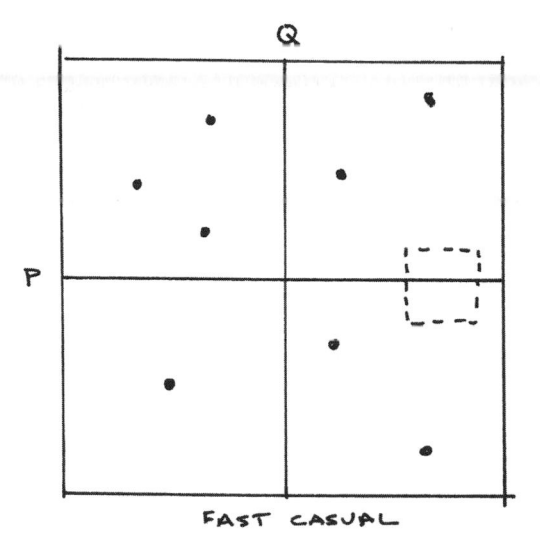

Figure 8.2 Initial Target Marketplace Chart for Start-Up

phones in the early 2000s, would you have seen those icons on the displays? Would you have stared at those icons and said, "What are mobile applications?" Would you have noticed the early, clumsy-looking protective cases?

For that matter, would you have guessed that people might some-day do their daily fitness run with a device strapped to their arms? Today, there are a large number of wearable fitness devices that meas-ure the distance run and calories burned.

You can apply this type of analysis or thinking to every new prod-uct or service you see enter a marketplace that you might care about. Almost all new products or services will have a relatively small impact at first (even the first Apple iPod was not considered to be successful in its first year). But some of these products will create entirely new industry segments—and therein lies tremendous opportunity.

The Perfect Storm...Trends Crossing Customers and Industries
The holy grail of entrepreneurship opportunity is uncovered when a major shift occurs across a large target population and simultaneously

that same trend is changing or impacting a large industry. For example, think of the demographic of 16- to 30-year-olds consuming content on their laptop computers and at the same time the distribution of content is dramatically shifting.

Think of those previously mentioned 78 million baby boomers buying pets to replace their college-age children and the simultaneous changes to the pet industry—pet health insurance, pet-tracking devices, organic FDA-approved dog food, dog-walking/sitting services for condo owners, new types of kennel services. These are times when customer developments and industry changes coincide. The trend/industry "intersection" line is there, can you see it?; see Figure 8.3.

All kinds of opportunities exist for a host of new companies. Consider that next largest segment of the U.S. population, the 18- to 35-year-olds, the millennials. Look at the trends they are shaping or are being affected by. Whether it's music, fashion, technology, food, or entertainment, they are disruptors. If the current companies in these marketplaces don't step up and listen to this large group of customers,

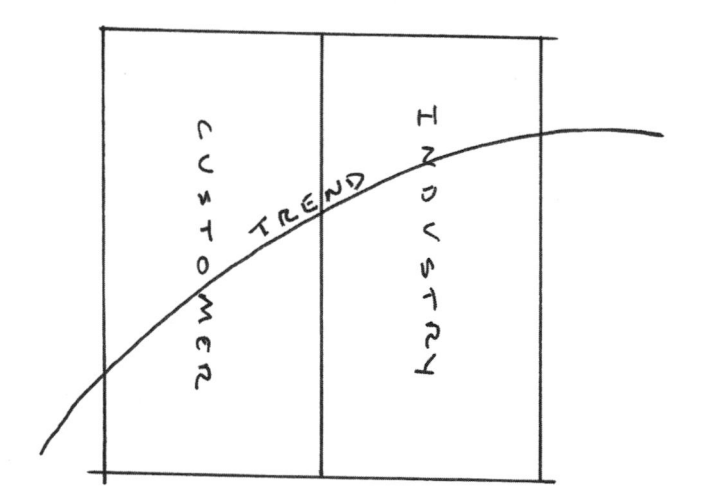

Figure 8.3 Perfect startup scenario: When trends cross target customers and industry in the same marketplace.

don't really understand the impact of their potential on forthcoming trends, then they will be rendered irrelevant. That's an opportunity for entrepreneurship.

ENTREPRENEUR INSIGHT

Sometimes there is a price to be paid for not seeing trends correctly. In early 1997, our marketing agency was in the middle of "blowing" up Amazon.com via the perfect intersection, albeit early, of customers, industry, and a trend called e-commerce. I attended a major book publishing trade show event to get a better understanding of how traditional competitors were looking at this new online world. After taking in a variety of workshops and events, as well as visiting company booths and listening to speakers, I found it apparent that the industry was ignoring the online sales potential. I stood next to the CEO of a major company and asked his opinion about the nascent online book industry. He replied, "We know what the customers want and we are building 25,000-square-foot stores to accommodate them." Then the CEO of Border's walked away.

KEY TAKEAWAY

There is opportunity all around you. Examine the marketplaces that are emerging, growing, or being disrupted. Couple your curiosity with passion and gather as much information as possible on customer segments so as to see the opportunity clearly. Then act on it.

CHAPTER NINE

Entrepreneurs Who Tried to Fail Fast and Won Big

There are a lot of reasons some start-ups try to *fail fast and win big*, while others simply fail. Sometimes it's marketplace timing, simply being too soon or too late. Other times, the idea is right but the execution is so poor the start-up fails. Perhaps the idea was right but the product didn't work or had quality issues. Some entrepreneurs never really design a business model that makes sense for the business. Others just can't get their distribution strategy right. Finally, some entrepreneurs just can't sell the product or service.

> *"Don't worry about failure; you only have to be right once."*
> —**Drew Houston, co-founder of DropBox**

Some entrepreneurs literally do everything mostly right but just don't have the courage to be relentless in sales. Sales drive everything. However, there are several traits that successful entrepreneurs share.

First, they are passionate about the problems they are solving or the opportunities to change an industry. Second, they may have years of experience in the same or similar industry. That is, they have what is called *domain knowledge or expertise*, meaning they have a skill set and knowledge base that allows them to understand the product very well. Third, whether consciously or not, they see the trends in the marketplace that will affect millions of potential customers. And fourth, they are not afraid to fail. I have discussed fear of failure in Chapter Five, but I encapsulate it here: You have one life to live and your own fear is what's holding you back—from what? Trying to build something in this world and have it not work is not failing; failing is not even trying.

For the start-ups that succeed and grow to be successful companies, most people do not know what actually happened early on in their development. They see a big brand or a successful company and they assume that all companies are either overnight successes or failures. Nothing could be further from the truth.

The very early days. That's often when some start-ups get going and others go away. In order to give you some extra insight, I profile here seven companies and their start-up experiences to provide a varied backdrop in both type of products and founder diversity.

There are reasons these companies tried to *fail fast* but instead *won big*. A key point to remember, though, is that it's not always about *winning fast*. Some of these companies took years to reach a critical point—perhaps they were just a little too early for an emerging marketplace. But it's what they did during their "early years" that offer insights that will, I hope, help you in your early years.

KASHI, THE HEALTHY CEREAL

While most of you know Kashi as a major brand today that is owned by Kellogg's, you may not know much about its beginnings. The company was started in 1984 by a husband and wife team, Philip and Gayle, in La Jolla, California. At that time, almost all cereals had too many preservatives and high amounts of sugar. There were almost no offerings for a nutrient-rich, healthful cereal that featured whole grains.

Kashi's founders were inspired by the notion of eating healthfully and were influenced by an Asian guru who had introduced to them the idea of a macrobiotic diet, as well as natural foods, holistic healing, and sustainable ways of life. Indeed, the macrobiotic movement introduced and popularized organically grown whole foods and naturally processed foods. The founders set out to launch a company that would create and introduce healthy products to the marketplace. They experimented with several types of grains and eventually settled on a cereal with seven grains and sesame seeds. One minor note, though. Before a person could eat the cereal, he or she needed to cook it, which could take 25 minutes. The founders thought that this was a fair tradeoff for the opportunity to eat healthier food.

They visited local bankers in search of funding, but the bankers did not fully support the product or the business model. The bankers were skeptical that consumers would take the time to cook the cereal and they worried that the founders did not have realistic expectations for product distribution. The bankers also knew very little about the coming revolution in healthful eating. So, every meeting with local bankers resulted in the same answer: Sorry, we can't loan you the money. This is the point at which most start-ups go away. How much money are you prepared to risk? Do you believe that you can pivot, duck, and run to find early adopters and influencers, and somehow make it to a larger market?

Then Philip and Gayle made the decision to risk their entire life savings of $25,000 and start the business. Next, they had to find a way to actually produce their cereal. They convinced a local manufacturer to give them 90 days of credit to produce the initial recipe, and then they negotiated a deal with a factoring company that agreed to buy their accounts receivable invoices for 92 cents on the dollar to help them resolve cash-flow problems.

The founders introduced their new cereal to the local marketplace. Remember, there was no Whole Foods at this point in time. Targeting friends and family, and independent health food stores, they found the initial response disappointing. People liked the product but complained about the lengthy cooking time. The founders were dismayed. They faced two choices: move forward and find a marketplace solution, or give up and lose the $25,000 they had invested.

This was another key point in time for Philip and Gayle. They knew people needed to eat healthier. They knew their product was healthy for people. They decided to move forward. The only problem now was customers. A key pivot here was to look beyond consumers for the moment and research who *served* healthful food. After a number of investigations, they started selling their whole-grain cereal mix to health spas. Based on some aggressive inquiry and personal relationships, they were one of the first companies to engage in product sampling at sporting events, where they distributed samples of their cereal (such as at the Olympic Games in Los Angeles). Slowly, a small but powerful following started to emerge. Athletes, trainers, diabetics, dieticians, vegetarians, and people suffering from heart problems began to form a core group around the Kashi brand. This core group, although small in number, slowly expanded and the Kashi cereal sales provided the founders with just enough revenue to keep the business afloat.

The overriding factor in the company's development was the founders' solid belief that people wanted and needed to eat healthful food. It just made such logical sense to them, and that viewpoint began to pay off. Unbeknownst to the founders, there was another entrepreneur in Texas who also recognized the growing trend in eating healthier. But he and the founders of Kashi faced a similar problem. The big food companies dominated the shelf space at large grocery stores. In the mid-'80s, even if you had great product, the dominant food companies and major retail grocery chains could essentially keep you out of that marketplace.

So, the entrepreneur in Texas came up with a better distribution strategy that would begin to support and drive a major shift in the emerging health, natural, and organic foods market. The entrepreneur would unite independent health-food stores into a national brand, and Whole Foods was born. As Whole Foods grew into a national brand and opened branches in California, Kashi had survived long enough to see a new distribution channel—one that aligned with their ideals. This new channel was funneling customers to their stores and that, in turn, gave Kashi a legitimate and direct distribution outlet that served health-conscious consumers. Sales began to climb, and that allowed Kashi to introduce several new products, including cold cereals. Sixteen years after the company was started, the founders sold their brand to Kellogg's in 2000. That's not exactly *winning fast*, but they did *win big*.

The Lessons Learned

- Believe in your product. Not foolishly, but with common sense. The founders believed that eating healthier food was good for people. Can't argue with that belief.

- Find ways to get things done and leverage everything you can to conserve and extend your cash flow.

- Follow the trend. Even though they were a little early to the health-food trend, they found other early adopters who believed in their products.

- If traditional distribution channels won't embrace your product, find other outlets or niche businesses that do. Look to alternate sources of distribution.

- Seek out other people or companies that have the same beliefs, and look for either leverage or distribution opportunities.

WEBSENSE—INTERNET FILTERING/SECURITY

To better understand how Websense got its start, you have to examine the background of its founder. A perennial tinkerer with a technology background, Phil had crafted a career as a computer programmer. His years of technology expertise paid off in 1994, when a little thing called the Internet was just starting to get noticed. One of the first things he noticed was that, as people and companies erected websites on the Internet, they were going to need some technical support. He looked at the infrastructure of the Internet and determined something those customers would need: secure firewalls and network security products.

These products were being offered by current software companies, but also by a rapidly growing set of start-ups. So Phil created a company called NetPartners, and resold other people's software products to this growing industry. Since he had no products of his own, he became a certified reseller and offered consulting expertise to companies still trying to grasp this new Internet technology. Business was steady but slow, as lots of other resellers rushed in to support this growing marketplace.

Over the next year, Phil observed companies rushing to put their websites on the Internet without really understanding the consequences of those actions. They not only needed tools and software to *get on* the Internet but also the management tools to maintain the sites. Specifically, as thousands of new companies built their websites, "surfing the Internet" became an employee-management issue. Market research would determine that as much as 30 to 40 percent of an employee's time was spent on the Internet for personal reasons.

Being technically savvy, Phil saw this problem and determined the solution was simple: create a network-based filtering program that would basically *outlaw* certain websites, based on their URL. Thus, NetPartners created its first product, the Websense Internet Screening System. This new software would allow system administrators to block access to websites based on which categories they were willing to pay for in their software subscription. (This was probably one of the first uses of a Software as a Service, or SaaS, subscription business model.)

The company began to grow and established a good reputation with IT managers and systems administrators, who told their CIOs that this kind of product was a *mandatory purchase* if the company wanted to manage Internet access by its employees. Phil had bootstrapped NetPartners from nothing to about a $6 million business by 1998, but he needed more resources to drive the development and sales of the company's Websense software product. So he gave up some equity and brought in about $6 million in venture capital. This allowed the company to refocus its resources on software development and away from being a reseller of other companies' products.

In 1999, Phil changed the company name to Websense and continued to pour resources into the development of other Websense products. And in early 2000, the company underwent an initial public offering. Websense was now a full-fledged software company, no longer the reseller of other companies' products.

The story of Websense sounds simple, but it's not. Let's look at the facts. The founder was *not* a savvy business person, he was a programmer. He had not acquired senior management expertise nor had he been involved in the creation of other companies. But he did have a deep understanding and curiosity of technology, especially software. Upon seeing the Internet, he probably just thought it was logical that people were going to need security products, and noticed that resellers of Internet technology were nascent and not really more knowledgeable than he was. So, with no other experience in business, he created a reseller company and bootstrapped that to $6 million in just four years. That's pretty amazing.

The more important realization from our founder was the identification and software solution that became Websense. In other words, he went from being a reseller of products to a real software company. And that is no simple pivot or transition. So what was the sole reason he felt the company would be successful? His deep understanding of technology and watching employees and consumers. He studied the Internet infrastructure and found the weak links. In May 2013, Websense was acquired and taken private for $906 million. The real win was in just those first four years.

The Lessons Learned

- Develop a deep expertise about something you love or are passionate about. The founder's technology expertise really-paid off several times in this journey.

- Notice a trend but have no product? Create a first company to create a second company. The founder, by jumping in and becoming a software reseller with little investment, learned a lot about the marketplace and was able to grow a business. After just two years, he saw a big opportunity and created a company that became an industry leader.

- Know when to pivot. The founder in the early days was still just reselling products when he developed his own product. Within just 18 months, that product was driving most of the company's revenue. He abandoned the reseller business and focused every resource on building Websense products. That focus exploded the Websense product line and revenue.

STONE BREWING—CRAFT BEER

The first time I met Greg he was speaking to students on the San Diego State University campus. An entrepreneurship student organization had invited him and I will never forget what he said about one minute into his talk: "People who drink beer deserve to drink real craft-brewed beer, not fizzy, pissy yellow beer from big companies that really don't care." I thought, *Who is this guy?*

The two founders of Stone Brewing, Greg and Steve, were from different backgrounds but they shared passions for two things: music and beer. One had owned a music studio and the other played in a band. They saw each other intermittently for a few years, then in 1994, at a beer-making course at a local university, they rekindled their mutual passion for craft beer. To get insight and experience,

Steve headed off to work at a growing craft brewer in another state, but they regularly kept in touch and discussed crafting their own beer.

Two years later, they decided to actually work together and began to experiment brewing different beers. When they thought they had a good beer—what would become Stone Pale Ale—they looked around for investors. They raised enough money from friends and family to purchase a 30-barrel brewing system. So, as Steve continuously improved and crafted the recipe, it fell to Greg to sell the beer. Since they were just starting out, they would need to sell their beer in kegs to local bars and restaurants. So, Greg used a small hand-held keg that he could carry and offered samples to bar owners and managers. "Most of them wrinkled their noses and said, 'No, thanks,'" recalled Greg.

Powerful and bitter, with a full hoppy taste, Stone Pale Ale was ahead of its time. It had arrived years before the hoppy, bitter India Pale Ales, or IPAs, would become popular. However, in the mid-1990s in the United States, the craft beer industry was growing rapidly with brands like Sierra Nevada, Boston Beer Company (Sam Adams), and New Belgium Brewing Company (Fat Tire and Blue Moon). At the same time that Stone Brewery got off the ground, I was in Portland, Oregon, leading the launch of Widmer Beer into bottles and into national distribution. So, even though I did not know anything about a little company named Stone Brewery that was getting started about 1,200 miles south, I was very aware of the exploding craft beer industry. In just two years, we quintupled the revenue of Widmer Beer with a successful launch into bottles and now onto grocery shelves.

So, if the industry segment was expanding, what was the challenge for Stone Brewery? Two things. First, to sell your beer at a local pub or restaurant via keg (draft), you had to unseat someone else's draft beer from the tap. Second, when you've got a distinctive and bitter beer, you have to convince people that your beer is better than others. Greg was relentless in his pursuit of selling the beer, meeting with as many potential customers as possible. But with no money for marketing, it was just one person, one sale at a time. Through the rest of 1996 and on into 1997, there were losses every month. The founders needed another round of investment. Again, friends and family came through—but this might be the last time.

In 1997, Stone Brewery released its Arrogant Bastard Ale, and some people would say the name reflected the founders' attitude. But when you build a brand, you either stand for something or you don't, and these guys were telling the world: "We are crafting beer the way it is supposed to taste." The local community responded to both their messaging and their craft beers, as they started turning a monthly profit for the first time in early 1998.

Now they had another problem. Sales were climbing, but they could not get a local beer distributor to carry their products. What was their solution? They bought a van and began distributing themselves—which, by the way, once you get enough volume, is way more profitable, as you've cut out the middleman. They poured every dollar back into the business and focused on making great craft beer. They had absolutely no money for any traditional marketing. In short, having no money for marketing meant they needed to be creative. They crafted a gargoyle logo and gave their beers memorable names. They talked at local events, especially about not drinking "yellow pissy beer." They donated their beer to local charity events to get more exposure. And they painted their delivery van with the smirking gargoyle logo.

In those early days, these guys worked harder and longer hours than their competitors, and continued to make beers they felt were true craft beers. Today, Stone Brewery sells more than $100 million of its craft beers throughout the United States, with plans to go abroad.

The Lessons Learned

- When you meet someone who shares the same passions as you, stay in touch.

- If you don't have enough expertise to create a company in an industry you are passionate about, then get that experience at an existing company in the industry, perhaps a future competitor.

- Selling is hard. Even though an industry is growing, there is limited shelf space. You just have to want it more than the next company.

- Creating great products may or may not be hard. Getting people to embrace them is another story. Be prepared to tell stories and convince people you have a better product that they actually will want.

- Building a brand when you have no marketing dollars means the brand is both you and your values. The founders, arrogant or not, believed so strongly in their product that they crafted a brand and an identity that showcased those beliefs. Great craft beer. In your face.

ecoATM—RECYLE YOUR PHONE

It was at a local networking event in San Diego that I met Michael, one of the founders of ecoATM. I knew nothing about the company. As we chatted, he talked about his wireless background and the fact that he had been in several start-ups, and they had just launched ecoATM. I asked, "What does your new start-up do?" I expected to hear about some cool new wireless company. Instead, he said, "It eats phones."

In late 2008, three wireless industry executives—Michael, Mark, and Pieter—each experienced in either starting or growing technology companies, would gather every week at a local coffee shop to talk about opportunities for a new start-up. (Remember, we were in the early stages of what looked like a pretty bad recession.) One week, one of the executives mentioned a recent survey noting that out of 6,500 U.S. households surveyed, only 3 percent of consumers had ever recycled a phone handset. At the time, there were perhaps a billion mobile phones shipping to customers every year. They asked themselves, "Where were all the old phones going?" As they discussed this problem, they saw two opportunities and one key benefit: (opportunity 1) recycle old phones and (opportunity 2) resell the phones that are still valuable elsewhere in the world. The key benefit would be to position the company as environmentally friendly.

Once they agreed that this was an idea worth pursuing, they started researching both the industry and the consumer marketplace. At their weekly meetings, they would each share what they had learned since the previous meeting. One key research fact that turned up was that the average U.S. household had six old cellphones, lying about somewhere in the house. After they had enough research data, the founders were curious to know if target consumers would actually recycle those old cellphones. So they sent an online survey tool to about 1,000 people. The result was that consumers wanted three key benefits to recycling their phones, or nothing at all. They wanted a financial incentive, the process had to be convenient, and they had to be assured that their personal data would be destroyed. The founders agreed that they had to come up with a solution that met these three criteria.

At another weekly meeting, one of the executives mentioned he had watched people at a local grocery store using a Coinstar machine to redeem their loose change. Could they design a kiosk or reverse vending machine that would take in an old cellphone and dispense cash? They all agreed a kiosk would meet their criteria. So, they spent the next few months researching various types of technology and kiosk business models. Since they really knew nothing about building a kiosk, they pooled their resources and used a local engineering firm to build a prototype. Not a finished kiosk, just a crude prototype.

Next, they tried to accomplish two tasks simultaneously. They reached out to anyone with connections to retailers to see if they could test their prototype. They also decided that they needed a reality check with venture capitalists. Knowing it would take serious capital expenditures to build future kiosks, they scheduled meetings with venture capitalists in Silicon Valley. Expecting to be laughed at, they were surprised when the venture capitalists liked the size of the idea (read: size of the marketplace) and encouraged them to get marketplace validation and feedback.

Amazingly, the first retailer who agreed to place the prototype kiosk outside its facility was a furniture store in Omaha, Nebraska. After only a few weeks, the word of mouth grew and people were waiting up to 45 minutes in line to trade in their cellphones and receive some cash in exchange.

Emboldened by the success of the test, the founders entered a variety of start-up "pitchfest" competitions, winning several that garnered them more than $35,000 in cash. A key move they made, however, was to attend and enter their kiosk prototype in a kiosk trade show competition in New York City, where they met the Coinstar founding CEO, Jens. Not only did they win the "best new concept" category at the trade show but they also built a strategic relationship with Jens. Riding the wave of public relations, which included an appearance on *ABC News*, they approached local venture capitalists and received a first round of funding. Included in this investment round was the Coinstar founder Jens. This added some serious legitimacy to their fledgling company. The funding would allow them to build several more kiosks and to begin crafting sales relationships with key partners. After two more rounds of venture capital investment and three years of growing marketplace success, ecoATM was purchased by OuterWall (formerly Coinstar) for $350 million in 2013.

The Lessons Learned

- Shared technology industry and start-up experience were what linked the three founders. Meeting regularly and looking at problems with corresponding but slightly different perspectives allowed them to see what anyone should have seen. Who do you meet with regularly?

- They stumbled on a big idea and a bigger marketplace. Yet they tested both with potential venture capitalists and customers.

- Building a crude kiosk prototype quickly allowed them to test the technology and observe people using the kiosk.

- Once they saw an industry leader in Coinstar, they made sure the leadership in that company would see their kiosk by attending a prominent kiosk trade show event.

- They carefully crafted a relationship with Coinstar's founder, who lent them instant credibility by investing in their start-up.

- By entering several "pitchfest" competitions, they drew both the local and national media's attention—free public relations.

ProFLOWERS—FRESH FLOWERS DIRECT TO YOU

While he was still in college in 1994, Jared created his first company, an Internet access, web hosting, and application service provider. The Internet was in its early days in 1994–96, but some people sensed that this was a game-changing technology. (Others looked at "cute" websites and probably said," Why do we need the Internet?") People like Jeff Bezos saw an infrastructure technology that enabled greater sales. Even though this college student would not launch ProFlowers for another four years, Jared was embracing the Internet technology and seeing its opportunities very early on.

After he graduated from college, Jared moved back to his home in Boulder, Colorado, to help manage sales at his family's greeting card and publishing business, Blue Mountain Arts. It was not long, though, before he suggested that the company build its brand by going online. Shortly thereafter, he launched the website BlueMountainArts.com, and started his marketing efforts in hopes of expanding the business. As he looked at what people bought online and in brick-and-mortar stores, especially for the holidays, he could not help but notice that people bought lots of flowers for all kinds of occasions. He started doing research into the flower market. How many flower arrangements were sold each year? Where did the flowers come from? Who were the middlemen who delivered the flowers to the independent florists? Why did flowers last only three or four days? The founder examined the industry giants who seemed to supply the world with flowers and studied their business models.

When he had gathered enough information, he made several key observations. The first was that the growers of flowers made very little money. Even though Colombia supplied about 75 percent of the world's roses, growers in that South American country made the least percentage in the actual transaction. The second was just how many of the flowers sold in the United States were imported. The third observation was how long it took flowers to get to a customer from the time they were cut. Yet another observation was that 70 percent of all roses sold in the United States were sold on Valentine's Day. This last bit of information would prove to be critical in the launch of what would ultimately become ProFlowers.

The young man was convinced that he was on to something. He had always looked for efficiencies, and saw several in this potential start-up. However, he needed to test-market the concept. He located a flower farm that would provide him with 500 bouquets of roses. On February 13, 1998, through a web-based promotion, he sold all the roses and had the San Francisco Floral Market ship them to arrive for Valentine's Day. At only $29 a dozen, he undercut the current price of $50 by almost 50 percent. The concept test worked. He envisioned a whole new supply-chain infrastructure, and it would be very simple: customers order their flowers online and the growers ship the flowers on behalf of ProFlowers. There would be no middleman. The founder just needed some capital to build this new web brand and the supply chain.

Moving rapidly, Jared sold his interest in one of his earlier companies to raise the capital for this new flower venture. Then, just two months later, he launched the ProFlowers website. Initially, the marketing strategy was to promote the flowers to Blue Mountain Arts customers. (When he launched the BlueMountainArts.com website two years earlier, he hadn't intended to sell greeting cards online. He wanted to build the brand to drive retail card sales. But a funny thing happened. Since he had no products to sell online, he created electronic greeting cards—free greeting cards online. Over the next two years, about 54 million people either sent or received a Blue Mountain Arts e-card. This was the online database that he then used to launch ProFlowers.com in April 1998.) Now, 54 million people received an invitation to send someone flowers. The company grew rapidly over the next several years, and in 2003 he changed the name to Provide Commerce. In 2006, Provide Commerce was sold to Liberty Media for $477 million.

The Lessons Learned

- When you see a new technology or marketplace emerging, start something during those early days. Anything. Then leverage what you've got later on, when you know what you really want to build.

- Look for efficiencies in big markets. This founder always focused on business models that were more efficient than what was currently operating in the marketplace.

- If you can acquire online customers or visitors by offering something that costs you little, you can leverage that resource to offer something that produces sales. Our founder used a 54 million visitor database to launch his next venture.

- If you are curious about a large marketplace, dive as deep as the research will allow you to go. Our founder studied the flower marketplace, from the growers all the way to the final customers. In that deep study, he saw opportunity and efficiency.

- Be bold. The founder's test for Valentine's Day sales in 1998 created buzz and generated news coverage. It also showed the industry, and potential customers, that someone could deal directly with the flower growers. I am sure no industry CEO paid attention to what they probably saw as a promotional event; that same mentality was shown by Borders about Amazon.com in its early days.

WAHOO'S—FISH TACOS AND MORE

How do you avoid doing what your parents don't want you to do? Well, initially, you could try to do everything else. But sometimes you are a victim of your upbringing, you really are not passionate about what could be a great career (but boring to you), and you really want to enjoy life without actually having to have it feel like work. Well, the last part is tough. But what if you created something that you loved to do so it did not feel like work? It's hard to accomplish, but that's what the three founding brothers of Wahoo's did.

They were born to Chinese parents who had immigrated from China to Japan and then to Brazil, where they opened a Chinese restaurant. The brothers worked in the restaurant every day. It was not far from their home—just up one flight of stairs. In 1975, the family moved to Orange County, California, and their parents opened another Chinese restaurant. As the brothers were growing up, they frequented the beaches and became avid surfers. Their parents, who were working long hours, told them that they were going to college and would become successful professionals. The parents said that the restaurant business was not for them, and they should study hard instead. So, the brothers went to college. They studied law, medicine, and engineering, respectively. During their summer breaks, they traveled down to Mexico to surf and enjoy the fish tacos. They had never had this kind of fish taco before: fresh grilled fish, not deep fried, with a side of rice and beans. They loved these trips and looked forward to them every year.

The oldest brother graduated first from college and began his career as a doctor. The youngest brother was not yet in college. The middle brother took a slightly different path; he enjoyed his extracurricular college life so much that he was in danger of not completing his degree. After careful consideration, he switched his major from engineering to finance and subsequently received his finance degree. He accepted a position in an aerospace company, and worked there for three years, hating almost every minute of it. His only joy came from surfing trips to Baja, where he continued enjoying those fish tacos.

One day, after a great day of surfing at a popular beach in Orange County, the brothers emerged from the water and considered where to eat. They wanted some healthy food, nothing fried, and typical fast food did not appeal to them. They all agreed it was too bad there was no great local spot where they could get good healthy food. Like those fish tacos they had in Mexico. They agreed that a combination of Mexican/Brazilian/Asian fusion food would be amazing. Within the next two weeks they agreed to create a restaurant that would be patterned after the kind of food they enjoyed in Brazil and Mexico. They also agreed to serve the food in as healthy a way as possible— nothing fried, and with a lot of fresh ingredients. All they needed was money.

As hard as this must have been, they actually approached their parents and told them of their idea. Imagine their parent's reaction. The parents had toiled for years in their restaurant business so that they could send all three sons to college and their sons could live a more comfortable life as professionals. But amazingly, their parents agreed to give them the money to start their first restaurant. The brothers opened that first location in 1988, within minutes of the top action-sports companies in Orange County. They felt a kinship with the surfers and the surfing industry, and thought the restaurant, themed with a surf décor, would attract people like them—people who loved life, surfing, and good food.

While the youngest brother was still in college, the older two brothers opened the restaurant. Since they wanted to use the freshest ingredients, and they could not afford to have the fish and produce delivered, they went to the markets every morning for two years. They bought what they needed to operate the restaurant for that day and then prepared it. One brother focused on operations, the other on marketing. Their marketing efforts consisted of handing out stickers at surf contests and offering the winners free meals, efforts to drive traffic with a core surf and skateboard crowd.

Their efforts must have worked because the business started to grow. Based on the success of their first restaurant, they opened a second in Laguna Beach, California. And they made one of their best hires when they selected someone to manage the second restaurant. This manager, who would later become chief operating officer of Wahoo's, had been working as a consultant to local restaurants so he brought operations expertise to the business that would allow them to rapidly expand even more. He also negotiated a major credit line from a respected financial institution, which gave the business credibility in the industry. Today, Wahoo's has more than 65 locations in several states and continues to expand. The brothers are all active in the company (president, chief financial officer, and VP of marketing) and still surf.

The Lessons Learned

- Love what you do, do what you love. Because the brothers grew up in restaurants, they understood the business. If you are going to enter a competitive marketplace, know your business.

- Timing. In the late '80s, there was a strong movement in California to eat more healthfully. Wahoo's was in sync with the surf and skater crowd, but also struck a chord with people who just wanted healthy food at a reasonable price.

- Recognize something unique and special in one part of the world and see if it would make sense to introduce it in another part of the world.

- Get ready to work. The most successful entrepreneurs have worked hard to get what they deserved.

VOLCOM—ACTION SPORTS LEADER

This action-sports brand was created by three founders who immersed themselves in a surfing and skateboarding culture at an early age. By the time they were in their early 20s, they were in the midst of the action-sports industry. In 1989, Richard worked in marketing for Quiksilver, which had gone public in 1986. Tucker worked in sales for Quiksilver, and Thom was a graphic designer who had created a marketing agency focused on youth brands.

All three met while surfing and witnessed other surfers who donned suits and ties or "business casual wear" at companies like Quiksilver and O'Neil. They watched shoe brands like Van's grow and seemingly sell out. But all three realized that this surfing/skateboarding culture, while aspirational and lifestyle oriented, was becoming a large marketplace with quite a few brands that they admired.

A key event that started Volcom occurred on a skiing trip to Lake Tahoe. The marketing guy, Richard, at Quiksilver was specializing in creating films to showcase the surfing industry, and by the early spring of 1991, he was headed to Tahoe with the sales guy, Tucker, from Quiksilver (who had just been laid off but came along for the fun) to check out this new thing called snowboarding. They were going to create a short film highlighting this emerging action sport.

The two were somewhat taken aback by the snowboarding scene at Tahoe. Here was a raw and unapologetic scene of snowboarders who were full on "punkers," with a rebellious and anti-establishment attitude. As skateboarders in the city streets, they had been harassed, viewed by residents and the police as nuisances. Now that they were on the mountain, the ski resorts were turning anti-snowboarding and actually banning the activity at some resorts. The expert snowboarders were tired of "the man" and all the rules; it was visceral and raw, and it felt like a revolution in the making. But with more than 50 inches of fresh powder that weekend, Richard and Tucker were snowed in for two days. And it was during these two days that a lot of ideas got thrown around for creating a new action-sports brand that would encapsulate the rebellion they were seeing and feeling. Volcom was being born.

Instead of going back to work, Richard called his boss and told him he was staying on the mountain for another week. Two weeks later, he quit Quiksilver. He asked his father for help, and with a $5,000 loan, the company was started. Richard and Tucker now sought out a third founder, Thom, the graphic designer who started crafting their brand, "youth against establishment." After some trial and error and countless designs, Thom designed the Volcom "stone" that has become the brand's iconic logo. Now the three founders divided their duties in this fledgling start-up, at that time being run out of the bedroom of the founders' Richard would focus on product development and distribution, Tucker on sales, and Thom on branding and marketing.

The only problem was that they had no product. No cool designs that could represent the brand. But they liked the logo and the brand it represented. So they made up stickers and began to distribute them to friends, surf and skateboard enthusiasts, and even delivered them to local skateboard and surf shops. No product, just stickers. For almost a year. Amazingly, it created buzz in the community, and eventually they launched the start-up with a few initial t-shirt designs.

They began selling their products out of their cars at surfing and skateboarding events. Running the company more like a cause than a business, after the first year they had sales of only $2,600. As they started to run out of funds, Richard's father, the original investor, stepped in: "If you don't get your act together, you are going to be out of business in about three months. I am not going to help you or bail you out. So, you better figure it out."

It was a wake-up call. They went to work getting more orders from local stores. They attended trade shows and took orders for products they didn't even have. They assembled one of the best snowboarding teams possible, including some professionals from Japan. Snowboarding was taking off in Japan, and this was a potential link to a Japanese distributor, who they arranged to meet at a trade show event. As a result, this Japanese distributor placed a $32,000 order. The only problem was that Volcom did not have the cash to produce the inventory needed to fill that order. The distributor agreed to make a deposit up front so that they could produce the product order.

The founders were amazed. Even though they were positioning Volcom as a new kind of brand across all action sports, it was the snowboarding market that would propel Volcom forward. They finished their second year with over $171,000 in sales. Volcom was on its way to becoming a valuable brand and, more important, a real company.

Over the next few years, the three founders dealt with growing problems. They applied the competitive discipline they had developed for surfing competition to business matters. They created a strategic plan and stuck to it. They resolved operational and production problems with determination. Instead of being just a surfing brand or a skateboarding brand or a snowboarding brand, Volcom was growing *the* brand that united all action-sports enthusiasts under the motto "youth against establishment." As the industry grew, so did Volcom. In fact, it grew right through an initial public offering in 2005. In 2011, a European company bought Volcom for $607 million.

The Lessons Learned

- Being an expert and having industry knowledge matters, even if it's skating, surfing, or snowboarding. What are you an expert in?

- When you see something that looks like an emerging trend or a revolution, see if it has legs and can be leveraged. Volcom leveraged "punk" snowboarders into the beginning of a solid brand.

- Anyone can create a brand. Few people can create a company. Both have to be aligned with customers who care. To create a company, you need sales.

- ABM—always be marketing. The fact that Volcom was distributing logo stickers for one year without product is kind of crazy, but it did create a buzz.

- Learn from your environment. All three founders watched and worked with companies like Van's and Quiksilver as they grew from their cult-like beginnings to being big companies. So, while it might be challenging to create a new company, it was not "foreign" to its founders. They lived inside the industry and witnessed "normal" people creating companies with almost nothing but pure passion. What are you passionate about?

CHAPTER TEN

If You Want to Be an Entrepreneur, Be One

There are a lot of books out there on entrepreneurship, as well as countless seminars you can attend. Not one of them will make you an entrepreneur. As I look back on my career and think about the hundreds of entrepreneurs I have met, and I consider what led me to become an entrepreneur, I see several interwoven threads. These threads have run through this book, but let me recap.

One, you have to be an expert or be amazingly passionate in your marketplace or industry. Remember the comment in Chapter Eight that it takes 10,000 hours to become an expert in any one area?

*Experts get more choices and more
opportunities. What are you an expert in?*

Second, you have to develop a tolerance level of measured risk. If you are young and don't have much, then you have nothing to risk, so to speak. If you have a strong skill set and are an expert in some field, you can always craft that expertise for someone else, so why not take the risk? If you fail, you can always go back to being a highly paid employee.

After nine years of building my marketing career, I left a highly paid job to take a risk in creating a new kind of integrated marketing agency. If we failed, we could always go back and do what we were doing before. But how did I reduce my risk? I knew the industry. I had a highly developed marketing skill set.

Third, it takes an amazing team to create a great company. When I met the other three people who would eventually become my partners, I really took the time to understand their strengths and weaknesses and how I could complement the team. Trust within the team is so critical. Regardless of what kind of business you eventually build, trusting your partners, which initially can be trying, is so important to the success and growth of the company.

Fourth, in order to be successful, you have to be willing to work harder than anyone else, harder than you've ever worked before. I worked seven days a week for the first year of my marketing career, using weekends to learn how to use complicated computer systems that allowed me to create very insightful research reports . That made me one of the most valuable people in the agency. Thom McElroy, one of the founders of Volcom (see Chapter Nine), talks about how he worked two jobs for almost eight years before Volcom really took off. How hard are you willing to work?

* * *

I was not born to be an entrepreneur. In the first part of my career, I helped build a small company into a much bigger company with almost $30 million in revenue. It was a private company owned by one person. As the company grew, other employees became disgruntled and wanted more of everything. They wanted more money, and they wanted equity in what was becoming a valuable company. They griped about it constantly. I finally told the people around me, "Get over it. It's the founder's company. He is not going to share it. If you want equity in a company, go create one and quit complaining."

Those employees continued to work for other people. While I was fine working for an entrepreneur who would never share his company with me, it planted two seeds in my brain. First, that I could create a company someday centered on my area of expertise, just as he had done. Second, that I could create a company with a team of people whom I respected and trusted, unlike this founder. So, in the first seven years of my career, I built my marketing expertise. In the next two years, I hunted for opportunities and for the right people. Funny thing is, when you know what you are looking for, you are apt to find it.

* * *

If you want to be an entrepreneur, consider what your area of expertise is. What is your skill set? Can you leverage your skill set in an industry or an emerging marketplace? What does an amazing team look like?

> *If you don't know where you are going, any path will get you there.*

I have met a lot of people who have become really good entrepreneurs. They are not special. What is the most important thing they do? It is that they *do*. They don't walk around posing like an entrepreneur and attend start-up weekends, playing a role. They quietly go to work on solving a problem or addressing the needs of a large marketplace. They surround themselves with good advisers and they are constantly seeking counsel and customer feedback. They have very little ego (don't mistake ego for confidence), and they believe the right (not necessarily best) idea *and* the hardest work ethic are what will win. They acknowledge that sometimes the reward goes to the team that just works the hardest. And so they don't easily quit. They adjust, evolve, and pivot. Sometimes this works and a company is born. Sometimes this does not work. But these entrepreneurs realize that there is no rewind in life, so they are definitely going to enjoy the ride. After all, if they fail, they can always go to work.

In this concluding chapter, I offer some final words of advice to all those seeking to be entrepreneurs.

BUILD A COMPANY TO FUND A COMPANY

Let's say you see a big opportunity in the marketplace but you don't yet have the capacity or the money to build the company you would like. What do you do? You build a company to fund a company. Here are two examples, one big and one small, that were mentioned earlier in the book:

- *Start with books, expand to retail e-commerce.* Jeff Bezos, of Amazon.com, had a big-picture vision. He wanted to build the largest e-commerce company in the world. He was starting with books, but his goal was to grow fast and acquire millions of customers. Once that goal was accomplished, he would launch the world's largest online retailer. The strategy worked.

- *Sell competitive products online to create real company.* Adam started out selling products online that matched competitive products in quality but at a 25 percent or greater discount. With about 100 products generating about $3 million in annual online-only sales, the company generated enough cash for the founder to create the solar products company he had envisioned a few years earlier. The new company is now branching beyond online sales into retail distribution, with its own line of branded unique products.

FOUNDERS CREATE START-UPS, TEAMS BUILD COMPANIES

Before I started building my career, I thought that any successful company just needed to have an amazing entrepreneur at its helm. That one person would know it all, had created it all, and was running it all. What I learned is that there is no such thing. Show me a founder who is a megalomaniac and I will show you a limited-options company. The very best entrepreneurs have a capacity for communicating a clear vision for their company and a passion to draw others to its mission. They have an ability to recognize talent when they see it, and have an amazing skill for recruiting people who share their passion. What true entrepreneurs realize is that they are only good at one or two things and so they need to attract the best possible people to help them in building a real company.

Here are the qualities and attributes of entrepreneurs who have the potential to build great teams:

- No ego but great confidence in themselves.

- Don't take themselves too seriously (Caesars need not apply).

- Have a great ability to communicate.

- Are good listeners because they ask great follow-on questions.

- Are not greedy; they realize everyone wins if a great company is created.

- Have an amazing work ethic.

- Understand what's important and what's not.

- Under fire, have an ability to stay calm (even if they are really not).

- Have an honest passion that draws people to them.

By no means is this a complete list, but these are the qualities that successful entrepreneurs display. Every now and then, I meet the rare entrepreneur, age notwithstanding, who seems so cocky and arrogant, that I wonder why they have to behave that way. That attitude and arrogance creates a negative aura that surely can't have enduring success. I think history has proved me right.

For those of you who have a great idea, and you want to build an equally great team, here is my advice for you in building teams:

- ABL—always be looking for great people

- Create the best possible diversified network you can; you will need it.

- When you think you found someone, do due diligence. You don't need to throw equity around; let people earn it.

- Put everything in writing; provide clear expectations and communication.

- Be a leader, not necessarily a tough manager; lead by example.

- Find people you can trust and build a team around them.

- Be honest with people; don't set them up for failure.

- Motivate and inspire people; no one wants to fail.

- Hold people accountable and make the tough decisions.

It's not going to be easy to build a great team and, I hope, a great company by yourself. Support and insights come from your network, advisers, mentors, work experience, personal values, and skill sets. Treat people the way you want to be treated. Don't worry about job titles, and be humble. Life is a journey, so at least enjoy the ride.

MENTORS REALLY DO MATTER

I did not have a mentor in my early days, when I was between 15 and 27 years of age. And I really don't have a mentor today. I just have really good people who I trust and who I go to for advice. But from the time I was 27 through about 45 years of age, three mentors propelled me toward the career I could only dream about in my youth. Their impact was everything on my life. They managed me, advised me, counseled me, praised me, and pushed me.

Everyone in life should have a mentor, at almost every stage of their career. It's invaluable. There are conversations, dinners, and ski trips that are etched in my mind as defining moments. I can honestly say I would not have had the career I did without my mentors. It's probably one of the reasons I am mentoring so many entrepreneurs today. My mentors "paid it forward" for me—they never really expected anything in return. That was amazing to me. Why did they care about *me*?

For a mentorship to work, something amazing has to happen.

Both people have to trust each other. Really deeply. Sounds easy, but it's not. I think it might be tougher to have a great mentor relationship than a marriage. Because this person will see you in ways your spouse might never see you. Most spouses don't see your faults in ways that could hurt your career. But you will have conversations with your mentor that will be almost clinical, kind of direct, and perhaps with some brutal honesty. Mentors will help you neutralize your weaknesses and expand your strengths. They will keep you from making "career-limiting" mistakes. They will be a great sounding board. They will make you think. They will hold you accountable. And, it is hoped, they will be your friend, even though that's a plus and not a necessity.

If you are in a career today or are looking to create a company, who is your mentor? If you don't have a mentor, don't just seek out someone who seems well respected or is well known in the community. Look for a mentor who will really help you in your career. That means the person needs to have deep experience in your career field or be an industry expert in an area where you are looking to launch a company. You want expert advice, not a new friend to show off. Get beyond your ego, and examine who you need around you to push and support you toward the next level of your life.

ENTREPRENEURSHIP IS A MENTALITY

I teach a creativity and innovation entrepreneurship course at San Diego State University, and in every class, the students are given a problem to solve. In most cases, they will have only 35 to 40 minutes to come up with a solution (they have to draw or build the solution), that they will then present to the class. We tackle both simple and complex problems. They have almost no resources, except for themselves, yet the solutions they come up with are amazing.

The student entrepreneurs I meet and mentor on campus also come up with really smart solutions to their problems. They are so resourceful because they have no money to solve these problems and so they have to be creative. They are already eating "mac and cheese" and ramen noodles; they know they are at the bottom of the ecosystem. They feel that they have nothing to lose, so they just run forward. They are not afraid to fail.

It's this same kind of lean mentality that you need to embrace as you start a company. You should be constantly in this state of mind regarding any and all resources. Because you probably won't have enough money to do everything you want to do. Your biggest asset is leverage, therefore. Leverage every resource possible, whether that's office space, technology, or people. Think lean, be lean. Guess what? If you behave in this manner, you will get things done and other people around you will become resourceful as well.

When I left my marketing agency assignment with Apple to join what would be my partners in the new company called CKS|Partners, I thought of all the benefits and perks I had working with Apple and with my previous marketing agency. Now, I pictured myself sharing an office in a building that used to be a prune-canning facility. There was no expense account. There was no private office. I was earning one-third my former salary.

What happens when this is your situation? You get hungry. You are hungrier than your competition. You work harder. You work smarter. Every dollar you spend is your own, so you spend less. We worked so hard and had so much fun that we built a $1 billion company.

So, assume you won't get enough—or any—money to launch your company. Accept that, and embrace it. Don't use it as a crutch or an excuse. Use it as an advantage that will move you faster. Leverage your way to creating some sort of prototype that you can test in the marketplace. Adopt a lean mentality.

EMBRACE THE IDEA OF LISTENING

An an entrepreneur you need to be constantly listening to your customers. The key is not to rely on customers to *tell you what they need*. Often they don't know. Or they might tell you what they want. I would never expect to have a customer tell me exactly what he or she wanted (or needed). But by spending enough time with customers, you can see what they don't want and don't need. Or, you can see everything that the customer loves or hates about the competition's products. Customer truth is your truth. Listen well and observe.

Customers are not always right but they are never wrong.

When you mention the name Steve Jobs, it polarizes people. Our agency worked with Steve for years at NEXT, Pixar, and Apple. Regardless of how you feel about him, he was insanely great at "being" the soul and voice of the customer inside Apple. Which means that he represented the customer to the Apple employees, the designers, and the engineers. He had a remarkable ability to spend time with customers or with competitive products, and to see the opportunities, again and again. Part of his talent was evident in his blending of customer insights and emerging trends. He was constantly interested in what was coming next, and he paid close attention to trends as they might affect customer behavior.

So, a collective customer voice is your truth. Ignore it at your peril. I almost feel sad when I think about the entrepreneurs who have tried to create companies but have absolutely ignored what their customers really wanted or needed. Their point of view was, "I created a great product or service, and if the customer can't see that, then I am just going to ram it down their throats." Of course, they failed—and they list myriad excuses why. The real reason? They did not know how to listen. They did not listen to their advisers, their employees, or their potential customers. The marketplace rarely has room for arrogance; put on your humble hat. Be prepared to adjust your product or service, based on feedback and changes occurring in the marketplace.

MARKETPLACES AND TRENDS YOU SHOULD WATCH

One of the by-products of my marketing career is an inability to stop watching marketplaces and trends. Most people don't see the trends forming all around them. But learn to spot these trends, match them to large marketplaces, and you can almost "see" the next product or service people will need.

If you saw Netflix in early 2000, would you have reasonably predicted the demise of Blockbuster? I say, yes. Consumer behavior was trending toward watching content on computer screens. Someone who is 25 years old or younger probably doesn't even watch television. They watch programs on a tablet, laptop computer, or their phone. Roku or Apple TV does not need a service repairman, or even a service van.

In no particular order, I present several marketplaces or industries to watch as opportunities linked to large marketplaces. You just need a big idea. Or a small one.

- *Pet Industry:* In the United States alone, the pet industry did more than $50 billion at the end of 2013 and it shows no sign of letting up. Plus, the trend is for parents to replace their college-bound children with pets. Over 150 million dogs and cats now live in the USA in about 78 million households. Throw in a desire for better food, smart technology, and urban-based services, and you have an industry that will be growing for the next 20 years.

- *Anything Cloud:* Standalone software is dead. Remote access to applications and services will not retreat. Email, social media, work platforms, e-commerce—everything cloud seems to be good. We will embrace smart cloud solutions that seemingly make our life better, but at what price? Oh, our privacy is gone anyway.

- *Big Data:* If everything we do is going into the cloud, and it's all online in one form or another, that's a lot of data. Who will turn that data into information? Who will create the smart "dashboards" that will make sense of it all? Several industry analysts claim big data will grow to more than $40 billion by 2017.

- *Wearable Devices:* We are simply fascinated by what we can monitor. Benefits in the future could be more predictive. Several fitness products in the marketplace today can give you important diagnostics on your heart rate and blood pressure. Products in the future will issue warnings based on your physical attributes and history. It's not that I want a text message saying I might have a heart attack based on my continued high blood pressure, but I do think I would appreciate it.

- *Remote Monitoring:* Our 78 million baby boomers are going to resist the idea of dying, but the most important trend is that they want to live in their homes as they age. That means local neighborhood care and video remote monitoring. Loved ones can gently "look in" and see that everything is okay. Wearable and monitoring devices alert health-care responders to an emergency. Seems like a fair tradeoff.

- *Smartphone Platforms:* These things we call phones are really some of the best computers ever developed. They are only going to get more powerful over time. That means other products and services (e.g., Square) will be designed to either reside on or "snap into" the handheld computer . . . er, smartphone.

- *Mobile Applications:* I don't want to sound smarmy or arrogant, but is anybody out there still designing software solutions for the personal computer? It's all mobile and it's all going on the smartphone. Niche and perhaps even disposable applications will do very well in the next 10 years.

- *Social Causes:* This one is my wild card. I'm not really sure how this area will do, but about 80 million millennials (by

2025) seem to really care about anything social, whether its clothes, shoes, or food. The environment and sustainability is big with this crowd, and they don't even have any power or money yet. Once they get the money and the power, that will change big time.

- *Healthy Fast Food:* The fast-food industry in this country is in trouble. McDonald's is on the down swing, while anything healthy, natural, and organic is on the rise. Millennials are not cooking as much and they are okay with eating on the go. Food trucks are popular (that will continue), but keep your eye on really healthy food prepared to go (or be delivered), and finished at home. That's way better than the frozen TV dinners of yesterday.

- *Rental/Sharing:* A 2012 *Wall Street Journal* study asked 500 adults between the ages of 21 and 30 what was the most important thing they could own. Choices included a home, a car, a smartphone. More than 80 percent of respondents indicated the smartphone was more important than a home or car. What does this mean? Millennials want to live now. They are going to treat life as a journey to be lived right now, and they won't wait for anything until retirement age. They are going to travel, eat, and dress themselves in the latest fashion. That's why services like Car2Go and Über will be commonplace over the next 10 years. What will we rent next?

- *3D Printing:* Another wild card. One industry analyst, SmarTech, estimates that the 3D printing market will reach $5.1 billion by 2018. If I had not seen someone actually use a 3D printer to recreate a door hinge (to replace a broken one), I would not have believed it. This industry will definitely grow. There will be 3D stores where people go and order something based on an image or drawing. Think Ceramic Café, but for 3D printing.

- *E-Commerce Niches:* We have really embraced e-commerce, and that is only going to continue. But I don't think Amazon.com has the market cornered. I have been following Etsy, and they are doing well. Companies that make "unique" things (Betabrand clothes, etc.) are doing just fine, too. The "niche" e-commerce companies who specialize and offer great products in certain categories can do really well.

Recommended Reading

People often ask me what I read. I read everything, voraciously. I still read the *Wall Street Journal* every day. And in addition to several magazine subscriptions, I have over 20 Google Alerts coming to me on different subjects every week. As I teach several entrepreneur courses at San Diego State University, I am constantly reviewing both textbooks and trade books written by either subject-matter experts or industry experts. I feel we can never give up on acquiring knowledge, and knowledge can best be acquired through either reading or doing.

There are books that have definitely had an impact on me and I consider them valuable, not just for entrepreneurship but also for understanding all those other elements that go into building a brand and a great company. I share them with you here.

Brand Gap, by Marty Neumeier. If you are an entrepreneur, you will need to understand what your company stands for and how it will be viewed and felt by your customers. I spent a good part of my life supporting, marketing, or creating brands. And it's not exactly the same thing as creating a company. While you can see the company, you really can't "see" the soul of a brand. That's because it's what your customers feel about your product that is most important. It's a great book that every entrepreneur should read before considering a name, logo, marketing message, or website.

Business Model Generation, by Alex Osterwalder and Yves Pigneur. This book was introduced to me by another professor at San Diego State University in 2011. The power and simplicity of generating and iterating a business model, with customers, to the point of failure as rapidly as possible, caused me to completely change my line of thinking as regards business plans. I now encourage potential entrepreneurs to forget writing a business plan and to use the business model canvas tool in this book. Period.

Don't Make Me Think, by Steve Krug. As an entrepreneur, chances are you will need to know a little bit about good user interface design, whether you're dealing with a website, a mobile application, or anything else involving interaction with a customer. This book was written by a designer for marketers, but every entrepreneur should read it as well. It will allow you to have intelligent conversations with user-interface designers and keep you from making big mistakes that could dramatically impact your company's revenue. Great book that is simply written with lots of pictures and examples.

E-Myth Revisited, by Michael E. Gerber. This book seems simple in its premise, but really helps entrepreneurs understand how they can *ruin* their new business. Its shows entrepreneurs what their role is in the company, particularly what they are good at and what they are not good at. It's a solid read if you are considering becoming an entrepreneur or an entrepreneur struggling with your responsibilities in your current start-up.

Founders at Work, by Jessica Livingston. Entrepreneurs should read this book just so you understand that nothing goes exactly as planned in a start-up company. And to adopt a philosophy of being ready to pivot based on listening to the marketplace and customers. Having helped launch Yahoo! and Amazon.com in the very early days, I can tell you we were constantly changing and revising our plans. By reading how some other well-known start-ups had major issues and pivots may give you a little reassurance before you descend into the chaos of a start-up.

How to Win Friends & Influence People, by Dale Carnegie. My first mentor must have noticed my complete lack of communication skills and networking grace. Not only did he make me read the book but he also sent me to a six-week class. It changed my life on how I communicate and network with people.

Positioning: The Battle for Your Mind, by Al Reis and Jack Trout. Most people never really understand how marketing, positioning, and branding actually work. This book does a great job of helping you to understand that it's not what you actually say or show to customers that matters. It's what you make customers *feel*. And their chapter about how to create a new category ladder in a competitive marketplace is invaluable to an entrepreneur.

Search Engine Marketing Inc., by Mike Moran and Bill Hunt. In meeting with a CEO/founder of a search engine marketing start-up in late 2008, I noticed he had a stack of more than 100 copies of this book behind his company's reception desk. I asked the CEO why he had so many copies of the book. He told me that every single employee, vendor, partner, board member, and adviser was given a copy of this book. He called it the bible for understanding search-engine optimization. He was right. Every entrepreneur will be impacted by search-engine results and needs to read this book before doing anything online.

Spin Selling, by Neil Rackham. Early in my marketing career, my second mentor took me aside one day and said quite bluntly, "You don't know how to sell." Then he did something amazing. He sent me to a weekend seminar on spin selling and it changed my life. I began to see my family, friends, clients, and professional associates differently. As an entrepreneur, your ability to understand multiple people types and to really grasp the difference between wants and needs is critical. This book will help you become so much better at getting people to want to buy from you, as opposed to your selling them something.

Tipping Point, by Malcolm Gladwell. As a marketing expert, I learned how important it was to have your new product or service focused initially on a group of early adopters or influencers, and that they would influence others to consider purchasing the product.

Reading this book gave me additional insights into what has to happen, to whom, in order to create a "tipping point" in the market, the place where the product or service takes off. Companies like Google and Facebook, both of whom did no marketing in the early days, benefited from understanding how targeting early influencers could really drive market adoption of a product or service—to the point where mass-market users learned about the product with essentially no marketing. Good book to read, as it will help you understand the ecosystem of potential users in a marketplace and how to create a potential tipping point.

Index

About the Author

Bernhard Schroeder brings over 20 years of marketing and entrepreneurial experience, both as a senior partner in a global integrated marketing agency and as a former chief marketing officer on the client side. Today, Bernhard is a Director at the Lavin Entrepreneurship Center at San Diego State University, where he oversees all of the Center's undergraduate and graduate experiential programs. In 2014, San Diego State University was ranked at number 18 on *Forbes* most entrepreneurial universities list. He has worked with hundreds of start-ups in the San Diego area, on and off the campus; he is a strategic adviser/mentor to several start-ups; and he is quoted frequently in both local and national media and has spoken at TEDx events. He also teaches several entrepreneurship courses (Creativity and Innovation, Entrepreneurship Fundamentals, Business Model/Plan Development for Entrepreneurs) within the College of Business Administration at San Diego State University.

Since moving to San Diego in 1997, he has specialized in working with entrepreneurs and venture capitalists in either growth or turnaround opportunities, with several companies ranging from $10 million to $150 million. Prior to moving to San Diego, Bernhard was a senior partner in the world's largest integrated marketing communications agency, CKS|Partners, which in 1998 had offices in over 30 countries, more than 10,000 employees, and over $1 billion in revenue. He joined CKS in 1991, when the firm had only 21 employees and just $2.5 million in revenue. He opened the first out-of-state agency office for CKS in 1993 in Portland, Oregon; and working with the other partners, grew the firm to almost $40 million in revenue by 1995, and led CKS to a successful initial public offering that same year.

Bernhard has marketing, operational, and entrepreneurship experience working with Fortune 100 firms like Apple, Nike, General Motors, American Express, Mercedes Benz, and Kellogg's, as well as start-up companies. He was involved in the initial branding and marketing launches for online companies like Yahoo!, Amazon.com, Corbis, and ESPN SportsZone; and the agency worked with many key brands like Levi's, Audi, Williams-Sonoma, McDonald's, United Airlines, eBay, Pixar, Timberland, Harley-Davidson, Microsoft, and Visa.

Connect with Bernhard Schroeder at www.bernieschroeder.com.